THE EXPLOITATION OF THE
MODERN-DAY ATHLETE-STUDENT

PLANTATION
EDUCATION

Rashad McCants

FOREWORD BY MARY WILLINGHAM

POST HILL
PRESS

A POST HILL PRESS BOOK

ISBN: 978-1-68261-828-8
ISBN (eBook): 978-1-68261-829-5

Plantation Education:
The Exploitation of the Modern-Day Athlete-Student
© 2018 by Rashad McCants
All Rights Reserved

Cover art by Aaron A. McCants, Aaron's Artwork
Cover design by Cody Corcoran

Post Hill Press, LLC
New York • Nashville
posthillpress.com

Published in the United States of America

DEDICATION

This book is dedicated to the nonbelievers. All of those who closed their minds to the possibility of real truth. To all my teammates, who stood against me in the one true moment of need. The one moment where brothers were needed to fight the good fight. I dedicate this book to you all. After these many years you all knew this was coming sooner or later. You all have great knowledge of the way I was treated while attending the University of North Carolina Chapel Hill(UNC-CH). You all knew we were at war. You all made it very clear whose side you were on. Now we must also share it with the world.

To all the coaches and administrators who stood by and said nothing after not only being a part of such an historic scandal, but also knowing the long-term damage and effect of academic misappropriation on athletes, students, and young black males in America. You should be ashamed. It should be hard to sleep at night and very difficult to live with the truth. Yet here we are.

To the media, who so desperately needed to cover up the truth about the American education system and the exploitation of college athletes simply because you profit and benefit from the stories and pain of athletes after we have fallen off our pedestal, where you so righteously placed us. You all will have an opportunity to shine your dim light on my book and pick apart all that's wrong with it, yet one fact remains forever. You all played a part in the biggest cover-up/scandal in college sports history, and no one is even speaking about it.

To the NCAA. The secret Cartel. The overseers. The Masters. The Owners. To those who openly possess college athletes as America's greatest workers on the new plantation of universities across the country. Who hide behind the shield of a logo. Who manipulate and dictate the lives of millions and millions of young kids annually with your mantra: No compensation. Free education.

To history, for allowing me to stand before you and present this masterpiece of information to the next generation of youth. Whether it's accepted or not, my writings are constructed from pure, positive intentions. To help His-Story become Our-Story. We should never want to change history; we should aspire to create a new story.

To my immediate family for your undeniable support. It's been a long, long road. Many of my relatives (you know who you are) criticize me secretly and smile in my face, the same as my peers. Mama, Daddy, Sade, Shanda, I love you all so much. This is for you. My first book.

I did this for all of you. So you can never forget my name. No matter the dirt, no matter the shine, when you hear my name, you know that it is only me.

To all the black athletes who will never read my book, due to the lack of ability to actually read it, I will make audiobooks available for you all. It is not your fault that the American education system failed you. Or, maybe it is. It's just too bad that no one will take accountability on either side of the coin, since not one of you stood next to, in front of, or behind me.

Trust me, I get it. You don't wanna piss off the fans. You don't wanna get your former coach fired. You just wanna do your thing and live your life. Trust me, I *get* it. In this book, you will also get it. I will attack your fears in the hopes of easing them so you can see that this never started with me. Best believe I will be the guy who fights alone. While you all watch from the windows.

CONTENTS

4th Quarter

FOREWORD

It was an honor and a true joy to work with college athletes at the University of North Carolina at Chapel Hill. I was consistently impressed with the persistence and resilience of talented young athletes who were dedicated to their sport and hopeful to use it as an avenue to improve their lives and the lives of their families.

I am very proud to have worked with Rashanda McCants and grateful to her for connecting me to her brother, Rashad. His willingness to go public with his athletic and academic journey at UNC was a game-changer. Rashad's act of kindness to support the future generation of college athletes was and continues to be both selfless and honorable. These are the same values that were once touted at the University of North Carolina at Chapel Hill, as the "Carolina Way." The 2014 ESPN interview with Rashad's teammates, Coach Roy Williams, and basketball analyst Jay Bilas, made it crystal clear that these values were something of the past. The silence of Rashad's teammates defined this turning point in Carolina's history, as they were summoned to go on camera to "support their school" after Rashad spoke out about rampant academic fraud. No one, except Rashad, dared to share their transcript. The players sat silently and obediently, in agreement with their coach, following the narration of his friend, the sports commentator. ESPN delivered us "fake news."

The NCAA is a cartel. Its member institutions are making money off the backs of vulnerable young people who are forbidden to speak out against a corrupt system. Following this obviously painful act of dishonesty, displayed for all to see, Rashanda, in her infinite wisdom, said, "The truth will always be the truth." The decisionmakers at Carolina chose to lie and cover up, and together with the NCAA, failed many athletes who were promised an education in exchange for their talent. Even the women's basketball advisor, and director of the UNC Center for Ethics, Doctor Jan Boxill, could not admit to a system that perpetuated social injustice through the promotion of educational fraud.

Without the athletes, however, the NCAA is nothing. College sport would cease to exist. The McCants' voices, along with those of other college athletes, are critical to impact change, both in the world of "amateur" athletics and in the education system. They are on the correct side of history. As I learned from my whistle-blowing experience, this is not easy. We need more voices. Rashad and Rashanda have paid, and continue to pay a high price, for speaking out against a system that perpetuates fraud.

As a reading and learning specialist, I know that the academic disparities that undermine the integrity of college athletics will continue to exist until we address the real issue. The underlying problem is the lack of literacy skills that some of our university-admitted students bring to the classroom. After working in the UNC athletic department for seven years, primarily focused on teaching basic literacy skills, I realized that the athletic program was jeopardizing the mission of education. Big wins, which bring vastly increased revenue, had become far more important than student learning. The students I was privileged to work with during my tenure in athletics at Carolina had real dreams of how they could contribute after their career in sports. I'm hopeful that this book will give people the courage to support current and future college athletes so that they receive the education they are promised, and deserve.

—Mary Willingham
Regional Literacy Director
KIPP Delta Public Schools

PROLOGUE

Originally created as an extension of higher education institutions, college athletics has become a multibillion-dollar business known for corruption and excess. One university that has illustrated this devolution is the University of North Carolina at Chapel Hill, where, for over two decades, students took hundreds of courses in African and Afro-American studies and independent studies that never met in a classroom setting. Nonathletes and student-athletes alike enrolled in these courses, and the majority of the athletes involved were football and basketball players. An internal audit into academic issues also showed evidence of unauthorized grade changes and forged faculty signatures.

African-American student-athletes who make up a higher proportion of UNC players, are disproportionately affected by the university's academic malpractice. Many have been led to believe that they can use college as a springboard for a professional sports career with minimal classroom engagement. The National Collegiate Athletic Association (NCAA) is under scrutiny and involved in several major lawsuits regarding compensation for athletes based on their commercial marketability and revenue generation for the universities. The NCAA has long advanced the argument that these players are paid in terms of scholarships and valuable education, but, to their dismay, the athletes often receive a less-than-adequate education that could even be described as fraudulent.

The NCAA has revised academic policies that encourage colleges to show that athletes are improving their academic performance while lowering their eligibility entrance requirements. Based on current NCAA academic policy, the institutions that fail to report an athlete's progress toward a degree each term will face penalties. These rulings were put in place in 2006, in response to a significant drop in the graduation rates of collegiate football and basketball players. In the years since the changes, many have expressed concern that the combination of heightened academic expectations and lowered entrance regulations would create an impossible situation for the campus employees responsible for providing academic support to athletes.

These support staff are asked to help a growing number of marginal students—potentially at all costs. Collegiate athletics, given its intersection with the educational and life outcomes of black male athlete-students, is indeed in turmoil. It's evident in the classic picture of a black male professional athlete with no degree, few post-career job opportunities, and used-up collegiate eligibility. The issue is also illustrated in the low graduation rates for African-American basketball players. Only about 55 percent of black players graduated in 2013, 25 percent lower than the graduation rates of white basketball student-athletes. Our United States educational system, and indeed our American society, has failed our youth.

Many African-American men's basketball players are leaving college without the proper educational degree or requisite skills to pursue a professional career outside of sports, a deficiency they often only understand years after they graduate. These issues are usually not caused by conspiratorial athletic directors, coaches, or faculty; instead, they are the unfortunate result of a system of fraudulent pathways that too often do not include a respectable college degree for student-athletes.

Within the football programs at the top 20 BCS (Bowl Championship Series) institutions, African-American student-athletes represent 5 percent of their student bodies, but 70 percent of the roster. The data clearly shows the limitations that U.S. colleges place on African-American and student-athlete academic achievement. Apparently, African-American students are good enough for the playing fields, but not for the scientific laboratories. It seems that, if colleges can build up African-American football players, they can also develop African-American historians, scientists, and teachers. If universities trained, recruited, and competed for African-American students in chemistry like they do in football, they could display Nobel Prizes alongside their Bowl Championship Series trophies.

Dr. Andre Perry, a contributing writer for The Hechinger Report and a David M. Rubenstein Fellow at The Brookings Institution, wrote in his 2014 article "Black Athletes Must Pick Up the Ball on Graduation Rates":[1]

- Across four quadrants, 55.3 percent of black male athlete-students graduated within six years, compared to 69.2 percent of student/athletes overall, 74.5 percent of undergraduate students overall, and 52.7 percent of black undergraduate men overall.
- 96.1 percent of these NCAA Division I colleges and universities graduated black male athlete-students at rates lower than athlete-students overall.

---

[1] http://hechingerreport.org/black-athletes-must-pick-up-the-ball-on-graduation-rates/

- 97.4 percent of these institutions graduated black male athlete-students at rates lower than undergraduate students overall.
- Indeed, academic irregularities related to athlete eligibility have haunted several U.S. colleges:
- Stanford (2011): Easy, convenient classes were withdrawn by academic advisors after years of being offered. Florida State (2009): Basketball and football players benefited from academic advisors taking their tests and writing their papers.
- Florida (2008): Current Carolina Panthers quarterback Cam Newton left Florida after facing possible dismissal for cheating.
- Memphis (2008): The NCAA exposed Derrick Rose's SAT scores as invalid, causing the basketball team to abruptly end their run to the NCAA Tournament finals.
- Michigan (2008): One university professor gave more than 250 student-athletes high grades from 2004-2007 in independent study classes.
- Auburn (2006): Academic advisors helped football players pad their GPAs in focused reading classes.
- Fresno State (2003): The men's basketball statistician and an academic adviser were caught in scheme wherein papers were written for athletes.
- Georgia (2003): Basketball players received inflated grades in a coaching class, which caused the university to withdraw from postseason play.
- USC (2001): The football and women's swim teams were sanctioned by the NCAA when it was discovered that tutors had been writing papers for athletes.
- Minnesota (1999): Tournament victories were erased for the basketball team after it was discovered that players had hundreds of assignments completed for them.

The roadblocks that constrain black male athletes as they seek specialized education for their chosen career path come from cultural forces and institutional structures that have unintended consequences. The first of these structural forces is the reality that many black athlete-students come to campus with a poor academic background and preparation. This disparity is often linked to the poor quality of urban public schooling in our nation, and it is amplified by recruiting practices and priorities that prioritize athletics over academics. Many of these black athlete-students come from high-poverty neighborhoods, and their transitions to college life are complicated by struggles like inadequate family support, personal expenses, and financial restrictions.

Basketball fans can't be trusted to demand better outcomes for black collegiate players, as their cheers for their favorite college team's quest for a Final Four, or a national title, drown out deeper ideals of student equity and education. Academic leaders can't be trusted either, as college faculty often view black athletes as unwitting accomplices of those who promote a runaway athletic agenda. Academic departments also often see themselves in competition with athletics for resources and attention. African-American athletes are generally not seen as worthy members of the academic institution, nor are they taken seriously in their pursuit of academic goals beyond athletics.

African-American athlete-students are categorized as merely athletes-on-campus to serve as entertainers for the rest of the university community. Black athletes and their nonathlete brothers and sisters have little leverage to change the situation because they lack natural political allies, on or off campus. But they actually hold some of the most powerful cards for changing conditions and creating more favorable outcomes for themselves and their teammates. The system, as it is now, provides tremendous incentives for high-profile college athletes to focus on sports rather than academics. Students from poor families face significant pressure to go pro early in order to better support their families. These financial pressures are pressing and urgent for black male athletes, who deal with the daily effects of poverty.

The combination of their personal athletic ambitions and encouragement from family and the campus community to set their sights on a professional sports career, leads athletes to view their futures as more tied to athletic performance than to academic achievement, and they set their priorities accordingly. Add to this mix the dire financial need of the athletes and their families, and the incentive to become an athlete with legitimate pro prospects is even more pronounced.

Other cultural issues for an athlete-student hoping to forge a path to the pros originate in the world of Amateur Athletic Union (AAU) basketball or other amateur networks. Talented players are identified early, promoted excessively, and given the type of access to shoe companies, agents, and college representatives that increases the opportunity for recruiting corruption. Underrepresented students can certainly benefit from this type of coaching and academic development when they are younger, but it is a pipeline that is also full of pitfalls, and it often sends athletes to college campuses with little preparation for the academic challenges they will face.

Simply enrolling in a college does not make an athlete a member of the academic community. If the academic side of the university is committed to retaining students of color, that mission must be accompanied by a resolution to reject the negative stereotypes about black male athletes. Under the current system, one could even say that generations of black athlete-students are being pushed in the direction of the postmodern-day slave: not enough education to read or write effectively, to understand contracts, to use critical thinking skills, to process bank statements, or to become independent entrepreneurs.

The NCAA has long claimed that the billions of dollars generated in college sports are the equivalent of a free education; therefore, athletes should not receive compensation for the entertainment they provide. But if the free education is flawed, then this system has been robbing college athletes of future opportunities for the past fifty years. Collegiate athletics bring in profits of some sixteen billion dollars a year, making athletes and fans alike wonder where those funds are used. Universities taking in the highest sports revenue boast the best facilities, accommodations, and reputations. To maintain this level of excellence, these universities must continue to fill seats with boosters, fans, and students, and attract top sponsors.

However, the University of North Carolina didn't provide academic benefits just to athlete-students, according to a three-month investigation into the scandal, which was headed by former North Carolina governor Jim Martin. Students in UNC-Chapel Hill's general population also benefited from special dispensations, like unauthorized grade changes, forged faculty signatures on grade rolls, and limited or no class time. "This was not an athletic scandal," Martin told UNC's board of trustees. "It was an academic scandal, which is worse."[2]

The independent investigation also showed that wrongdoings in UNC's Department of African and Afro-American Studies (AFAM) went back to the fall of 1997—earlier than originally reported. The review discovered 216 classes with proven or potential problems, including 454 unauthorized grade changes. Furthermore, the review stated that the percentage of grade alterations for athlete-students was consistent with student-athlete enrollment in those classes. "The athletic department, coaches,

---

[2]   http://www.espn.com/college-sports/story/_/id/8765672/north-carolina-tar-heels-investigation-reveals-academic-scandal-african-american-studies-department

and players did not create this," Martin told the board of trustees. "It was not in their jurisdiction; it was the academic side."[3] The review also unearthed evidence that employees of the UNC student-athlete support program were aware that certain courses within AFAM were so-called "paper courses" that were being taught as independent studies.

UNC's internal investigation found that fifty-four classes in AFAM were either "aberrant" or "irregularly" taught from summer 2007 to summer 2011. More than 50 percent of the students in the suspect classes were athletes. One summer class in 2011 had an enrollment of eighteen football players and one former football player. UNC said that no student received a grade without submitting written work. In August 2012, further questions were raised about the scope of the scandal when posters on a North Carolina State message board found a partial transcript of former two-sport UNC-Chapel Hill star Julius Peppers. The low grades and class choices revealed on the transcripts raised questions about how far back problems in the AFAM program extend. UNC-Chapel Hill, the investigation alleges, failed some of its students "for years" by allowing them to take classes that did not match its own academic standards.

Naturally, a story this electric would lead to questions for head basketball coach Roy Williams. When questioned at a postgame news conference, Williams said he agreed with the university statement that the claim was untrue and totally unfair:

> One important question concerning the UNC-Chapel Hill scandal is whether the issues raised by the university's internal report, and persistently

---

[3]   http://www.espn.com/college-sports/story/_/id/8765672/north-carolina-tar-heels-investigation-reveals-academic-scandal-african-american-studies-department

repeated and dissected by the media, are ongoing ones or simply past missteps that university leadership have acknowledged and addressed. In July 2005, reports surfaced that said Williams violated NCAA rules while coaching basketball at Kansas, allegedly approving payments to players who used up their eligibility, the school said Friday.

We all hear so much about corruption in college sports. We hear about players with no money tooling around campus in forty thousand-dollar cars.

We hear about fat-cat boosters smoking cigars, driving large convertibles, and giving talented players cartoon bags of money (complete with dollar signs on the canvas). And yet the reality is different. Anytime a "corruption in college sports" story breaks, there is no car. There is no Boss Hog being investigated. There is rarely even a big cash payment. Black athlete-students have no choice but to play a major role in their own success. They must take full advantage of the scholarships given to them, in spite of the obstacles they face in trying to get a quality education. Without a doubt, some athletes have to pay a political price to force institutions to cater to black males' academic talents.

If they hope to graduate with a degree that means something, black collegiate athletes will need to use the political leverage they have with the university—and be committed to finding a way to get more of their teammates to cross that graduation stage each year. African-American athletes can't wait for others in the university community to wake up to the issues; they have to pick up the ball. They must set aside the notion that they're just athletes and, instead, see college as a crucial step on their life's journey. The graduation rates suggest that many student-athletes are walking away from college after their future career in professional sports turns bleak. But if they make that choice…

…they will soon learn that the sidelines of life are cold.

INTRODUCTION

Finely tuned athletic machines, trained for collisions and acrobatic phenomena. The display of speed, power, and sheer spectacle. For the sixty-nine years that African-Americans have been allowed to play professional sports nationally, America has engineered a system of highly qualified, muscle-bound, barbaric, competent physical specimens, who by any means and without question, protect, promote, and preserve the exploitative and prejudiced intentions of existing slave owners, who have masterminded the Modern-Day Athlete.

The loyalty I have witnessed from athletes who have thrived within the university slave system occurred in my freshman year at UNC, when my coach was Matt Doherty. You would think that any player with a backbone would defend themselves against a coach's derogatory and offensive statements; however, I observed firsthand how a coach could belittle a player and make him feel like a kid. To this day, teammates, former players, and current players have remained silent about situations in which they were humiliated or made an example by the coach in front of the team.

I remember an account during my freshman year after a loss. Coach Doherty stormed into the locker room, disgusted with our performance, and immediately started pointing fingers at certain guys and blaming their performances for the loss. His tirade went something like this: *I'm gonna be here for a very long time, my job is very secure. But you guys* [pointing fingers] *are not secure. You all should just pack up your bags right now and go back home because you don't deserve to wear a Carolina uniform. I know you don't like what I'm saying but it's true. You (Raymond) can go back home and go to South Carolina State. You (Melvin) can go back home and go to Baltimore Community College. You (Sean) can go back home and go to Indiana State. You (Jawad) can take your ass back to Cleveland and attend Cleveland State for all I care. You (David) can take your ass back down the road to Durham. Because I don't need you. You need me.*

I'll be damned if all these guys showed up to practice the next day like nothing ever happened. They were laughing and joking with the coaches, yet I stood there as if we were ready to go on strike and not practice at all. I stood and waited to see if there was going to be any other player who felt, like me, that the statements issued by Coach Doherty the night before were completely inappropriate by any standard. It was that loyalty by the other players that blindsided me. I couldn't fathom the reasons that stood in the way of respect and obedience.

We all read stories of athletes transferring from schools for reasons of not getting along with the coaches, or clashing with the way the coaches treat players. I never questioned the *system* because I was always a different player from the rest. I always stood out as a natural leader and outspoken player. So, naturally I clashed with the *system* without having to question it, for it always questioned me. Even to this day, the *system* still questions why I won't just conform and play along like everyone else. When I decided to play sports, which was the one thing I always wanted to do, I decided that I was not going to take orders or change my identity. Never once did I agree to being exploited. However, there is no other avenue for the athlete who wants to take the independent route and make a life for himself with the talent he has developed. The only avenue available to athletes is sports. And if this is a way of life for them, then they must by all means comply.

But whatever you do, don't buck the system!

Athletes approach sports with magnified blinders in a sense that they see nothing but the sport. The outside world doesn't exist to them. Athletes enter university sports programs, certainly not for the glitz and glitter, because there is none. They're sold a bill of goods, a promise, a dream. They are misinformed about their future and misguided throughout their educational journey. Yet they continue to bite the hook that is held out for them with juicy bait—the allure of a quality education and making it to the pros.

It is the same for some fans in the way that they have made a life out of watching sports. The benefit for the athlete is the supreme admiration of peers, media, and fans that often tips into idol worship. There is a distinct difference between the common man and the athlete in the culture of sports. The common man is seen as the fan, and he looks up to athletes and adores them as superior beings with God-given talent. Most common men would die to have the ability to showcase such talent. The fan sees the attention and money made by the athlete as a gift from God or some universal spirit that gives out such gifts, with that "talent gift" having passed them up.

Another benefit of the athlete is access. As children, we grow up watching TV commercials and movies with athletes being able to appear and promote all the products, which the common man goes out of the way to buy, just to feel a little bit closer to the athlete.

We grow to idolize these athletes and their access. It is that vision that we want to embody with each and every step closer to the grand stage. This benefit creates an illusion of value to the athlete, who believes that this access and admiration lasts forever.

Little do they know that after sports can no longer benefit you, you can no longer benefit sports! And that value you once had becomes a memory as you are reintroduced to society outside of sports, where no one knows you or gives a damn what sport you played and how well you played it. Upon exiting sports, the athlete becomes a common man, thus losing his super powers or God-given talent that gave him promise. Without those powers, the athlete becomes the fan, the commentator, the coach, or just another citizen.

Therefore, it makes sense for an athlete to cling to this benefit and embrace its consequences because both seem to be a win-win for the loyalty of the common man and submissive athlete. If this life were all that is available to the athletes, why would they deny it? Why would they complain about it? Not unlike a slave who had been sleeping in mud huts, then later bought by another master and able to sleep in the big house, how is this not a better life for him? Even if he becomes a free man, he has already been conditioned to appreciate what has been given and not to appreciate what can be created. That's why it is never all-bad for the athlete. It's a decision. To be validated and given value rather than becoming valid and creating value.

***

The current generation of youth in sports and entertainment is in dire need of accurate information; there's a great misconception when it comes to what you can and can't do. I believe this book will open people's eyes on the social interaction among kids, young adults, and older adults. I believe there's a consciousness that needs to be awakened and shifted. This book will show young adult athlete-students that they can fight for a *real* education and *real* compensation. They don't have to exist as free laborers, falling for the fraud of contracts, the fraud of false promises, and the evil and corruption of the NCAA.

My ultimate goal is that your life will be changed because you'll have more awareness through reading this book. This is an important book for both parents and children. I believe this book is going to be somewhat of a cautionary Bible that can provide parents *and* young adults information on what steps to take, which college to go to, which coach to trust, which classes to take, which courses to follow through with, and how to evaluate scholarship opportunities and compensation, such as athlete-student eligibility to receive multiple scholarships—and more that may not be common knowledge to the average parent.

This book is not about me personally. The information I'm going to share with you is a necessity—to the world, to young adults, to their parents. If I don't do it, who will? Once you read this book and absorb the information, you will know that you have a choice. Without enough information, you don't have enough evidence to make an educated choice, but once you get the facts, you can weigh both sides. That's exactly what I want to do—give you the facts.

As I just explained, this book is not about me. With that being said, however, I will incorporate small dashes of my personal experience that fit into where I'm going with the story line. For example, if we're talking about the AAU circuit and how massive it is as an athlete's incubator, I will tell you how I got involved in it and exactly what happened to me. You'll read a firsthand account of how, at such a young age, it starts infiltrating a kid's life.

You might hate my guts, you might have preconceived views of who I am, or you might have let the media shape your view of me as a snitch or a traitor. That's fine with me. This book is based on my experience as a former athlete-student and professional basketball player. The content contains facts, data, and direct quotes from those surrounding the UNC athlete-student scandal, as well as other high-performers in the sports industry. My hope is that you'll read this book with an open mind, in order to learn, to perhaps shift your paradigm, to have a revelation about how you fit into the system, and to discover viable solutions to the athlete-student dilemma that already exist within the university and NCAA.. Throughout these pages, we'll take a look at how the *system* was devised, how it continues to operate under the radar, the problems associated with the *system*, and, finally, solutions where the athlete-student finally wins on all sides: academically, athletically, and personally.

The subject of this book is bigger than me and I'm very attached to the mission of sharing it with you. I'd put my life on the line for it. This is *real* philanthropy. It's about what you are standing up for. There are a lot of people who have said to me, "Yeah man, we know it's the right thing to do, but we just can't support you because we got too much to lose as far as resources and relationships." But my sister, Rashanda, and I, hand in hand, stood right in front of the fire. She's the only person who stepped forward and really supported me. Mary Willingham, Jay Smith, and Sonny Vaccaro have also been supporters during my journey.

When I went to Charlotte to play a game with the Big 3, a pro basketball league created by rapper/actor Ice Cube and entertainment executive Jeff Kwatinetz, I expected a lot more than I got. I got a couple of boos. I was expecting fans to storm the court. I was expecting people to throw drinks and food, to spit: I expected all of that. I got none of it. First, these people are kind of afraid of me. And secondly, they used to love me so much, so when they see me in the flesh, it's a whole different dynamic now. Because they remember me. *Oh my God, we remember him, that's him. Wow!* And in that moment, they forget what happened. I think the fans in the stands were kind of torn between what they used to love, pre-

UNC scandal, and what they still love, the adversity, and how I'm bothering what they love now. But they're going to remember the way they used to love, so there's going to be some backlash.

I'm so used to it, playing against NC State, playing against Duke, playing against any team where you have twenty-five points, and their teammates booing every time I got the ball prepared me for the negative fan reaction at the Big 3. So, I just kind of treated it as a neutral playing ground, where I'm not at home, I'm not away, but these people don't like that I'm shooting the ball. So, I didn't ever look into it deeper than I was supposed to. I thought, *Well, when you guys start throwing drinks on the court, then I'll start worrying, then I'll start paying attention. Then I'll look for my family.* But for a few boos, it wasn't that important. If it weren't for the support of my sister, Rashanda, as well as the professional support from Mary, Jay, and Sonny, I may have experienced a different reaction.

***

The coach and university did not fail me! I failed myself. The purpose of this book is to let everyone know just that, but it's also more than that. I want the next class of students to know that you have a choice now; you have a reference to consider when making your choice to move forward in life. I will decode the puzzle for you so that you can understand it in terms that make sense to you. You'll hear the story from me, the so-called *crazy, lazy, bipolar, "mad* because he didn't make it in the NBA," broke, snitch, traitor, who is willing to give you the truth about your million-dollar body and to tell you that you have more than a ten-cent brain.

What I tell you will allow you a glimpse behind the thick curtain of deceit and deception so deeply embedded within our society. The fraud, which is so much a part of the university/ NCAA system, is not the only issue. You'll learn that the way the *system* is set up is a much bigger problem than merely academics and athletics.

Thinking about my years at UNC, I can only blame myself for being young, ambitious, and totally clueless to the small print of my future. There was no one else accountable for the decisions I made. I can't blame anyone for the reason I'm writing this book or sharing my experience with ESPN. I can only blame myself; I am the reason this story must be told.

I was able to turn my million-dollar body into a irreplaceable portrait by an unknown painter. I can only hope that anyone who reads this book will feel the same sensation I felt as I wrote it... as we all sit back and watch a intellectual genocide of generations of youth blinded by rewards and accomplishments, validation and non-value.

1ST QUARTER

The Origins of Plantation Education

1

How far back does the exploitation of African-American culture go? To understand the plight of the modern-day athlete, we must first look back at the origins, where it all began, and why there is a generational system in place that continues to run strong, especially in athletics. In 1619,[4] the Dutch introduced the first captured Africans to America, planting the seeds of a slavery system that evolved into a nightmare of abuse and cruelty that would ultimately divide the nation.

Slavery in America started when the first African slaves were brought against their will to the North American colony of Jamestown, Virginia, in 1619. Slavery continued throughout the 17th and 18th centuries with African-American slaves helping to build the economic foundations of the new nation. Masters rewarded obedient slave behavior with favors, while rebellious slaves were brutally punished. Slaves were subject to a process called "buck breaking," a method that was used by slave owners to strike fear in the observing slaves. It is the process of brutally beating an individual in front of a group of people to incite fear and a sense of dominance. To further "tame" the U.S. slaves, a brutal, systematic breaking was put in place by Willie Lynch.

---

[4]   http://www.history.com/topics/black-history/slavery

Lynch was a British slave owner in the West Indies. He was invited to the colony of Virginia in 1712 to teach his methods to local slave owners. The term "lynching" is derived from his last name. See if you can identify parallels between some of Willie's methods and the modern-day slave owners (team owners, coaches, universities, and athlete-students, not to mention corporate America, and the entertainment industry). I've italicized a few select passages for emphasis.

The following speech is purported to have been delivered by Willie Lynch on the banks of the James River in the colony of Virginia in 1712.

The Willie Lynch Letter: The Making of a Slave![5]

December 25, 1712

Gentlemen:

I greet you here on the bank of the James River in the year of our Lord one thousand seven hundred and twelve. First, I shall thank you, the gentlemen of the Colony of Virginia, for bringing me here. I am here to help you solve some of your problems with slaves. Your invitation reached me on my modest plantation in the West Indies, where I have experimented with some of the newest and still the oldest methods for control of slaves. Ancient Rome's [sic] would envy us if my program is implemented.

As our boat sailed south on the James River, named for our illustrious King, whose version of the Bible we cherish, I saw enough to know that your problem is not unique. While Rome used cords of wood as crosses for standing human bodies along its highways in great numbers, you are here using the tree and the

---

5   https://archive.org/stream/WillieLynchLetter1712/the_willie_lynch_letter_the_making_of_a_slave_1712_djvu.txt

rope on occasions. I caught the whiff of a dead slave hanging from a tree, a couple miles back. You are not only losing valuable stock by hangings, you are having uprisings, slaves are running away, your crops are sometimes left in the fields too long for maximum profit, You [sic] suffer occasional fires, your animals are killed.

Gentlemen, you know what your problems are; I do not need to elaborate. I am not here to enumerate your problems, I am here to introduce you to a method of solving them. In my bag here, I have a foolproof method for controlling your black slaves. *I guarantee every one of you that if installed correctly it will control the slaves for at least 300 years.* My method is simple. Any member of your family or your overseer can use it. I have outlined a number of differences among the slaves and make the differences bigger. *I use fear, distrust and envy for control.*

These methods have worked on my modest plantation in the West Indies and it will work throughout the South. Take this simple little list of differences and think about them. On top of my list is "age" but it's there only because it starts with an "A." The second is "COLOR" or shade, there is intelligence, size, sex, size of plantations and status on plantations, attitude of owners, whether the slaves live in the valley, on a hill, East, West, North, South, have fine hair, course [sic] hair, or is tall or short.

Now that you have a list of differences, I shall give you an outline of action, but before that, I shall assure you that distrust is stronger than trust and envy stronger than adulation, respect or admiration. *The Black slaves after receiving this indoctrination shall carry on and will become self refueling and self generating for hundreds of years, maybe thousands.* Don't forget you must pitch the old black Male vs. the young black Male, and the young black Male against the old black male. You must use the dark skin slaves vs. the light skin slaves, and the light skin slaves vs. the dark skin slaves. You must use the female vs. the male. And the male vs. the female.

You must also have you [sic] white servants and overseers distrust all Blacks. *It is necessary that your slaves trust and depend on us. They must love, respect and trust only us.* Gentlemen, these kits are your keys to control. Use them. Have your wives and children use them, never miss an opportunity. If used intensely for one year, the slaves themselves will remain perpetually distrustful of each other.

Thank you, gentlemen.

Let's Make a Slave

It was the interest and business of slave holders to study human nature, and the slave nature in particular, with a view to practical results. I and many of them attained astonishing proficiency in this direction. They had to deal not with earth, wood and stone, but with men and by every regard they had for their own safety and prosperity they needed to know the material on which they were to work. Conscious of the injustice and wrong they were every hour perpetuating and knowing what they themselves would do. Were they the victims of such wrongs? They were constantly looking for the first signs of the dreaded retribution. They watched, therefore with skilled and practiced eyes, and learned to read with great accuracy, the state of mind and heart of the slave, through his sable face. Unusual sobriety, apparent abstractions, sullenness and indifference indeed, any mood out of the common was afforded ground for suspicion and inquiry.

Let us make a slave. What do we need? First of all, we need a black nigger man, a pregnant nigger woman and her baby nigger boy. Second, we will use the same basic principle that we use in breaking a horse, combined with some more sustaining factors. *What we do with horses is that we break them from one form of life to another that is we reduce them from their natural state in nature.* Whereas nature provides them with the natural capacity to take care of their offspring, *we break that natural string of independence from them and thereby create a dependency status, so that we may be able to get from them useful production for our business and pleasure.*

Cardinal Principles for making a Negro

For fear that our future Generations may not understand the principles of breaking both of the beast together, the nigger and the horse. We understand that short range planning economics results in periodic economic chaos; so that to avoid turmoil in the economy, it requires us to have breath [sic] and depth in long range comprehensive planning, articulating both skill sharp perceptions. We lay down the following principles for long range comprehensive economic planning. Both horse and niggers is no good to the economy in the wild or natural state. Both must be broken and tied together for orderly production. For orderly future, special and particular attention must be paid to the female and the youngest offspring. Both must be crossbred to produce a variety and division of labor. Both must be taught to respond to a peculiar new language.

Psychological and physical instruction of containment must be created for both. We hold the six cardinal principles as truth to be self evident, based upon the following the discourse concerning the economics of breaking and tying the horse and the nigger together, all inclusive of the six principles laid down about. NOTE: Neither principle alone will suffice for good economics. All principles must be employed for orderly good of the nation. Accordingly, both a wild horse and a wild or natur[al] nigger is dangerous even if captured, for they will have the tendency to seek their customary freedom, and in doing so, might kill you in your sleep. You cannot rest. They sleep while you are awake, and are awake while you are asleep.

They are dangerous near the family house and it requires too much labor to watch them away from the house. Above all, you cannot get them to work in this natural state. Hence both the horse and the nigger must be broken; that is breaking them from one form of mental life to another. *Keep the body take the mind! In other words, break the will to resist.* Now the breaking process is the same for both the horse and the nigger, only slightly varying in degrees. But as we said before, there is an art in long range economic planning. You must keep your eye and thoughts on the female and the offspring of the horse and the nigger. A brief discourse in offspring development will shed light on the key to sound economic principles. Pay little attention to the generation of original breaking, but concentrate on future generations.

Therefore, if you break the female mother, she will break the offspring in its early years of development and when the offspring is old enough to work, she will deliver it up to you, for her normal female protective tendencies will have been lost in the original breaking process. For example, take the case of the wild stud horse, a female horse and an already infant horse and compare the breaking process with two captured nigger males in their natural state, a pregnant nigger woman with her infant offspring. Take the stud horse, break him for limited containment.

Completely break the female horse until she becomes very gentle, whereas you or anybody can ride her in her comfort. Breed the mare and the stud until you have the desired offspring. Then you can turn the stud to freedom until you need him again. Train the female horse where by she will eat out of your hand, and she will in turn train the infant horse to eat out of your hand also. When it comes to breaking the uncivilized nigger, use the same process, but vary the degree and step up the pressure, so as to do a complete reversal of the mind.

Take the meanest and most restless nigger, strip him of his clothes in front of the remaining male niggers, the female, and the nigger infant, tar and feather him, tie each leg to a different horse faced in opposite directions, set him afire and beat both horses to pull him apart in front of the remaining nigger [sic]. The next step is to take a bull whip and beat the remaining nigger male to the point of death, in front of the female and the infant. Don't kill him, but put the fear of God in him, for he can be useful for future breeding.

***

I must interject a personal story here to exemplify a modern-day Willie Lynch mentality.

During my freshman season at UNC under Matt Doherty, I had the best first five games since Michael Jordan and Joseph Forte. The fans and media hailed me as the savior of UNC, also known as "blue heaven." At the time, I was averaging 21.2 ppg (points per game) and leading the Atlantic Coast Conference (ACC) in scoring as a freshman. We had just landed back in Chapel Hill after winning the preseason NIT tournament, where I was named MVP. You would think that everyone would be excited and celebratory from our victories and starting the season 5-0 after an 8-20 season the previous year. Wrong!

There was one guy who was very unhappy with how things had panned out: Matt Doherty. He called me into his office the day after we had arrived back to campus. I didn't know what to expect, but I presumed "Coach" would offer me personal congratulations or something like that. As I entered the coach's office, however, I was greeted with a cruel, smug look as he sternly told me to sit down. He reached into a drawer in his desk and pulled out a small magazine that looked like a *TV Guide*. He slammed it on the desk, glared at me and said, "This is not your team. This is *my* team. You know who you remind me of? Michael. He used to walk in the locker room like he was hot shit. None of us liked Michael. Coach Dean [Smith] didn't even like Michael. That's why Michael never averaged over 20 points a game." Coach made it clear that Michael was *not* the team. Coach continued, "So if you think for one second you're gonna come into my program and become like this selfish asshole, you got another thing coming. Your teammates already don't like you. I'm not even sure I like you. But I can guarantee you I'll teach you whose team this is. I'll make sure you never reach the likes of an asshole like Michael. Do you understand me?"

In a state of confusion and awe, I finally looked at the magazine on the desk and it was me on the cover. At that moment, I sensed Coach's jealousy. This was the start of my breaking. I had shown myself to be the best player on the team, who garnered the most attention. It was time for him to show me who was in charge. Later in the season, I was benched for three games while I was still leading the ACC in scoring and being talked about as a "one and done" player. The "one and done" rule allows young players to enter the NBA draft after just one year of college play. My average went from 22 ppg to 17 ppg. It was the first time I cried since I was a child. It almost broke me completely. *Almost.*

Now…back to Willie Lynch.

***

The Breaking Process of the African Woman

Take the female and run a series of tests on her to see if she will submit to your desires willingly. Test her in every way, because she is the most important factor for good economics. If she shows any sign of resistance in submitting completely to your will, do not hesitate to use the bull whip on her to extract that last bit of resistance out of her. Take care not to kill her, for in doing so, you spoil a good economic. When in complete submission, she will train her offsprings in the early years to submit to labor when they become of age. Understanding is the best thing.

Therefore, we shall go deeper into this area of the subject matter concerning what we have produced here in this breaking process of the female nigger.

We have reversed the relationship. In her natural uncivilized state she would have a strong dependency on the uncivilized nigger male, and she would have a limited protective tendency toward her independent male offspring and would raise male offsprings to be dependent like her. Nature had provided for this type of balance. We reversed nature by burning and pulling a civilized nigger apart and bull whipping the other to the point of death, all in her presence. By her being left alone, unprotected, with the male image destroyed, the ordeal caused her to move from her psychological dependent state to a frozen independent state. In this frozen psychological state of independence, she will raise her male and female offspring in reversed roles.

For fear of the young male's life she will psychologically train him to be mentally weak and dependent, but physically strong. Because she has become psychologically independent, she will train her female offsprings to be psychologically independent. What have you got? You've got the nigger women out front and the nigger man behind and scared. This is a perfect situation of sound sleep and economic. Before the breaking process, we had to be alertly on guard at all times.

Now we can sleep soundly, for out of frozen fear his woman stands guard for us. He cannot get past her early slave molding process. He is a good tool, now ready to be tied to the horse at a tender age. *By the time a nigger boy reaches the age of sixteen, he is soundly broken in and ready for a long life of sound and efficient work and the reproduction of a unit of good labor force.* Continually through the breaking of uncivilized savage nigger, by throwing the nigger female savage into a frozen psychological state of independence, by killing of the protective male image, and by creating a submissive dependent mind of the nigger male slave, we have created an orbiting cycle that turns on its own axis forever, unless a phenomenon occurs and reshifts the position of the male and female slaves. We show what we mean by example. Take the case of the two economic slave units and examine them closely.

The Nigger Marriage

We breed two nigger males with two nigger females. Then we take the nigger males away from them and keep them moving and working. Say one nigger female bears a nigger female and the other bears a nigger male. Both nigger females being without influence of the nigger male image, frozen with an independent psychology, will raise their offspring into reverse positions. The one with the female offspring will teach her to be like herself, independent and negotiable (we negotiate with her, through her, by her, we negotiate her at will). *The one with the nigger male offspring, she being frozen with a subconscious fear for his life, will raise him to be mentally dependent and weak, but physically strong, in other words, body over mind.* Now in a few years when these two offspring become fertile for early reproduction we will mate and breed them and continue the cycle. That is good, sound, and long range comprehensive planning.

Warning: Possible Interloping Negatives

Earlier we talked about the non-economic good of the horse and the nigger in their wild or natural state; we talked out the principle of breaking and tying them together for orderly production. Furthermore, we talked about paying particular attention to the female savage and her offspring for orderly future planning, then more recently we stated that, by reversing the positions of the male and female savages, we created an orbiting cycle that turns on its own axis forever unless a phenomenon occurred and resift positions of the male and female savages. Our experts warned us about the possibility of this phenomenon occurring, for they say that the mind has a strong drive to correct and re-correct itself over a period of time if I can touch some substantial original historical base, and they advised us that *the best way to deal with the phenomenon is to shave off the brute's mental history and create a multiplicity of phenomena of illusions,* so that each illusion will twirl in its own orbit, something similar to floating balls in a vacuum.

This creation of multiplicity of phenomena of illusions entails the principle of crossbreeding the nigger and the horse as we stated above, the purpose of which is to create a diversified division of labor thereby creating different levels of labor and different values of illusion at each connecting level of labor. The results of which is the severance of the points of original beginnings for each sphere illusion. Since we feel that the subject matter may get more complicated as we proceed in laying down our economic plan concerning the purpose, reason and effect of crossbreeding horses and nigger, we shall lay down the following definition terms for future generations.

Orbiting cycle means a thing turning in a given path. Axis means upon which or around which a body turns. Phenomenon means something beyond ordinary conception and inspires awe and wonder. Multiplicity means a great number. Sphere means a globe. *Crossbreeding a horse means taking a horse and breeding it with an ass and you get a dumb backward ass long headed mule that is not reproductive nor productive by itself.*

Crossbreeding niggers mean taking so many drops of good white blood and putting them into as many nigger women as possible, varying the drops by the various tone that you want, and then letting them breed with each other until another cycle of color appears as you desire. What this means is this; Put the niggers and the horse in a breeding pot, mix some assess and some good white blood and what do you get? You got a multiplicity of colors of ass backward, unusual niggers, running, tied to a backward ass long headed mule, the one productive of itself, the other sterile. (The one constant, the other dying, we keep the nigger constant for we may replace the mules for another tool) *both mule and nigger tied to each other, neither knowing where the other came from and neither productive for itself, nor without each other.*

Control the Language

Crossbreeding completed, for further severance from their original beginning, we must completely annihilate the mother tongue of both the new nigger and the new mule and institute a new language that involves the new life's work of both. You know language is a peculiar institution. It leads to the heart of a people. The more a foreigner knows about the language of another country the more he is able to move through all levels of that society. Therefore, if the foreigner is an enemy of the country, to the extent that he knows the body of the language, to that extent is the country vulnerable to attack or invasion of a foreign culture. For example, if you take a slave, if you teach him all about your language, he will know all your secrets, and he is then no more a slave, for you can't fool him any longer. *For example, if you told a slave that he must perform in getting out "our crops" and he knows the language well, he would know that "our crops" didn't mean "our crops" and the slavery system would break down, for he would relate on the basis of what "our crops" really meant. So you have to be careful in setting up the new language for the slaves would soon be in your house, talking to you "man to man" and that is death to our economic system.*

***

Another personal experience must be interjected here. There was one instance while I was playing for Roy Williams when, during practice, he kept getting a few of the players' names wrong.

At the time, there was Reyshawn Terry, Jawad Williams, and myself. He would mix us up and call us different names. One day after getting us confused multiple times, he stopped practice and said, "Dagnabit, why can't you be named Peter, John, or Billy?" I was in complete shock and my jaw literally dropped in the middle of practice. I looked at Roy and said, "My name is Rashad, Coach. And that's what you will call me." Seconds later we were on the line, running for my back talk.

Back again to Willie Lynch…

***

In addition, the definitions of words or terms are only a minute part of the process. Values are created and transported by communication through the body of the language. A total society has many interconnected value systems. All the values in the society have bridges of language to connect them for orderly working in the society. But for these language bridges, these many value systems would sharply clash and cause internal strife or civil war, the degree of the conflict being determined by the magnitude of the issues or relative opposing strength in whatever form.

For example, if you put a slave in a hog pen and train him to live there and incorporate in him to value it as a way of life completely, the biggest problem you would have out of him is that he would worry you about provisions to keep the hog pen clean, or the same hog pen and make a slip and incorporate something in his language whereby he comes to value a house more than he does his hog pen, you got a problem. *He will soon be in your house.*

***

There you have it. The world according to Willie Lynch. Unfortunately, that's the world according to many others in charge of the plantation.

See any similarities to the modern-day treatment of student-athletes? Any parallels? If you don't, you must be blind. There's a quote that aptly fits here:

There are none so blind as those who will not see.[6]

There are other examples of the slave mentality at work. John Henry, American folk hero—big and powerful, born a slave in the 1850s. The story portrays John working on the railroad as a hammerman once he became a free man. Million-dollar body with a slave mentality. A free man who still wants to work as a slave. This describes the athlete's state of mind, the Willie Lynch state of mind. This is what is expected of us. *You're going to fucking work and you're going to fucking appreciate it.* We are to never complain about the opportunities given by those in power. *Shut up, do your work, and your reward is to do more work…until your heart gives out.* Obedient athlete-student slaves are rewarded with more work, only to make more money for those who hold the power. Disobedient athlete-student slaves are punished by being psychologically and socially demonized by the slave masters in charge.

Nat Turner was the leader of the first slave rebellion, in Southampton County, Virginia, August 1831. He was God-sent to release the slaves from bondage, after his many attempts at escape finally built his courage to act and stop being afraid. Learning deeply about Nat Turner in African American studies (AFAM) courses helped me understand the importance of being outspoken about injustice.

---

[6]   Originally credited to John Heywood in 1546

My AFAM teacher during summer sessions was a passionate black man who resembled a Latino. Professor Arturo was his name and it was his passion for teaching that kept my attention during his lectures when he spoke about African-American culture. I had heard the Nat Turner story in brief prior to college, in American history class. But listening to Professor Arturo explain the whole story in detail was an experience in itself; he told the story as if he had been there. The most memorable part of the lecture for me were the signs from God that Nat received, which prompted him to gather slaves to begin the revolt. In the story, Nat explained that, while watching a few of his siblings get tortured, an epiphany came to him. He wondered, Why have you not risen? Why are you only a witness? The instructor explained that Nat's pain for his siblings had exceeded his control, and so he convinced others that they would be next if they did not act on their own pain.

Sitting in the professor's class as he related the Nat Turner story caused me great sadness as I thought about my ancestors. I would look around the class and find a white person to scold, searching for some sympathy for such abuse. These types of stories could only bring about rage in a seventeen-year-old who could not yet understand the choices that existed back then. The story continued as Nat described the simple plan: *we attack while they are all asleep.* And from house to house they attacked, as if every house brought them closer and closer to freedom and redemption. The rebellion was one of no longer settling for the slave role or standing by watching their siblings being killed and tortured. It was the word of God that prompted Nat's rebellion. But if the slave master tells the story, he would say it states in the Bible that slaves are just a part of society and that God prompted slavery, so I guess God just wanted some entertainment that week.

However, Nat Turner was caught and killed along with hundreds of other slaves who helped carry out the revolt. Even those who knew nothing about it were slaughtered. Widespread fear spread among all plantations around that time, and many say these events led to the Civil War. Nat Turner paid with his life. As soon as I heard the story of his accomplishments, I immediately viewed him as a hero and I can forever be grateful to Professor Arturo for sharing his story.

***

Almost a hundred years later, in the 1960s, resistance to the prolonged racism and discrimination in America that began during the slavery era prompted the civil rights movement, which achieved the greatest political and social gains for blacks since Reconstruction. However, the slave mentality that Willie Lynch spoke about was and is still alive and well on the athlete-student plantation. Exploitation of the African-American is nothing new to society, and the epitome of it all can be found in the academic/athletic arena called universities. The university plantations are run by predominately white "owners," with the majority of coaches being white; in fact, most of those in charge are white. The workers on the education plantation are predominantly black.

In professional sports, the term and associated connotation of "team owner" is still very much alive. However, the "team owner" owns the team as an entity; he doesn't "own" the players, yet the term itself is one of control. The players must "answer to the owner." It's the Willie Lynch mentality all over again.

We see the Willie Lynch mentality in full operation in the NFL Carolina Panthers organization, where, according to a recent article by *Sports Illustrated*,[7] owner Jerry Richardson *is referred to by all simply as Mister, no surname required.* The article goes on to state

---

[7]   https://www.si.com/jerry-richardson-carolina-panthers-settlements-workplace-misconduct-sexual-harassment-racial-slur

that even *if employees have already eaten their lunch, they accept any and all lunch invitations by "Mister." If "Mister" confuses an employee's name, that employee remains silent.* I'm perplexed as to why the employees don't just call him "Massa."

***

I would be remiss if I didn't discuss the origins of how the NCAA/university athletic *system* came about. It didn't happen overnight. Amateurism was first introduced in England, where middle- and upper-class men dominated the sporting world. The elite class wanted to block the professionalization of sports because it opened the door for working-class people to compete with success. There were opposing interests between those who wanted sports to be open to everyone and those who were apprehensive that professionalism might destroy the "Corinthian spirit" that was synonymous with wealth and luxury.

Fast-forward to 1906, when the NCAA was formed to create competition and eligibility rules for intercollegiate sports.[8] More than one thousand educational institutions are members of the NCAA. In 1951, Walter Byers,[9] the first executive director of the NCAA, coined "student-athlete," a term that was quickly implanted into all NCAA rulebooks. In his later years, Byers changed his paradigm and viewed the NCAA as working against the best interests of college athletes, enriching the schools and the coaches with hefty infusions of money while hiding behind the pretense of amateurism when it came to players' rights.

---

[8]   https://www.britannica.com/topic/National-Collegiate-Athletic-Association

[9]   http://www.al.com/sports/index.ssf/2015/05/walter_byers_first_ncaa_execut.html

In Byers' book *Unsportsmanlike Conduct: Exploiting College Athletes,* he ultimately acknowledged, "Against such an array of power stands the young athlete, unorganized and a part of the system for only four to six years before he or she moves on to be replaced by another 18- or 19-year-old. Whereas the NCAA defends its policies in the name of amateurism and level playing fields, they actually are a device to divert the money elsewhere." Surely a different tune from his original staunch defense of amateurism.

The term "student-athlete" came to the forefront of national attention from a case in the 1950s, when a player named Ray Dennison died of a head injury he sustained during a football game. The NCAA was involved in a lawsuit filed by his widow, who was seeking workers' compensation benefits. The NCAA used Byers' term "student-athlete" to prove that Dennison was not in a workplace when his injury occurred. He was essentially a volunteer. The Supreme Court of Colorado ultimately agreed with the school's contention that he was not eligible for benefits, since Fort Lewis A&M College was "not in the football business."[10]

Harry Edwards' book *Sociology of Sport* talks about the origin of collegiate sports and how the mob wanted to maximize their profits back in the 1900s, so they came up with the idea of creating sports within Ivy Leagues, and then extracurricular activities outside of the Ivy Leagues.

The first eight Ivy League schools were a breeding ground for sports betting, with football and baseball being the first sports that were controlled as gambling sports.

Originally, university sportsstarted as a way for politicians and mobsters to make money off extracurricular activities. Once they understood that university involvement would bring in more fanfare, they started building more stadiums, and ticket prices went

---

[10] https://deadspin.com/how-the-myth-of-the-ncaa-student-athlete-was-born-1524282374

from five dollars to ten dollars to twelve dollars. They saw the writing on the wall—their profit margin would increase if they built bigger stadiums and had more teams. With an influx of that much money, there have to be rules and regulations on how that money gets spent. The politicians and mobsters didn't want guys from outside cities coming to play for certain universities, so they started a scholarship program that allowed everyone to control who was going to be on what team.

It was soon discovered that medical insurance and workers' compensation would become an issue, and that's when the NCAA was created. The NCAA was basically like a fraternal plug that controlled who could go where, and how many could attend certain universities.

Basketball, football, and all the other sports became increasingly profitable for executives, politicians, mobsters, and the administrators of the universities. When sports were added to the university structure, an athlete-student had to be enrolled in the university to be a part of the sports program, which empowered the university and NCAA to exert more control over the athlete. When scholarships were birthed within the university system, that's when it became suitable for athlete-students to play for free.

It's well documented that the NCAA was a cover, a corporate cover, and a legitimate business cover for the mobsters. With the NCAA in place, the betting didn't have to be betting: it could be called *investments*. The mobsters invested in the universities as boosters and sponsors, as they would with dry cleaners, car dealerships, and other entities used as business fronts.

So, how did the mob-driven beginnings of the NCAA turn into the powerhouse of fraud and the mind-raping of college athletes as we know it today? Compromise, greed, apathy, and a deeply-rooted plantation mind-set, by those in power *and* the athletes themselves, slowly eroded the fiber from which universities operated.

College basketball corruption is also steeped within the mob-driven point-shaving scandal, as Bethany Bradsher carefully details in her book *The Classic: How Everett Case and His Tournament Brought Big-Time Basketball to the South*. Bradsher chronicles The Dixie Classic, played from 1949-1960, where NC State, Duke, Wake Forest, and UNC invited the top teams from the rest of the country to come spar with them. The tournament came to a screeching halt amidst scandalous revelations of point-shaving, first by the mob, and then by the players themselves. Fraud is fraud, no matter whether it manifests itself through point-shaving or through fake classes. Even though I experienced academic fraud, paper classes, and a severe "plantation education" mentality at UNC (which I will explain in detail), it's obviously not just at UNC; it's rampant among universities across the nation.

One extreme case is the Southern Methodist University (SMU) football program:

> On February 25, 1987, SMU received the only "death penalty"[11] ever levied by the NCAA. The school had been on probation six times since 1956, four times in the previous twelve years. Most of the violations involved offers of cash, cars, and jobs from SMU boosters. The decision of the Committee on Infractions, which was delivered by David Berst, NCAA director of enforcement, to more than one hundred reporters from around the nation, was hailed as the culmination of the message NCAA-member institutions sent in June 1985, when they passed the death penalty rule by a vote of 427-6.

---

[11] The death penalty is the popular term for the NCAA's power to ban a school from competing in a sport for at least one year. It is the harshest penalty that an NCAA member school can receive.

In his 2017 article, "30 years later: The legacy of SMU's death penalty and six teams nearly hit with one" CBS Sports' Dennis Dodd writes, "In the three decades since the death penalty, there have been fifty major infractions cases involving Division I-A/FBS football programs. In the previous thirty years before that, there were 102 such cases…BYU remains the only national champion free from NCAA sanctions in the wire service era (since 1936)."[12]

The five cases that have come close to the death penalty, according to Dodd's piece, are: Baylor (basketball, 2005); Penn State (football, 2012); Alabama (football, 2002); USC (football, 2010); and Oklahoma State (football, 1989).

Issues reported with these five death penalty cases include academic misconduct, drug testing policies, violation of ethical conduct rules, and impermissible academic extra benefits.

The academic fraud and paper classes I experienced at UNC had its genesis far before I arrived. Mary Willingham, former student advisor, worked in the Center for Student Success and Academic Counseling at UNC-Chapel Hill until 2014. Jay Smith is a professor of history at UNC, and coauthor (with Willingham) of *Cheated: The UNC Scandal, The Education of Athletes, and the Future of Big-Time College Sports*. They both have a lot to say regarding how the tangled web of academic fraud came to the forefront at UNC, and how race has always been a part of how universities and the NCAA catch their prey and exploit it for mega-profit.

According to Smith and Willingham, "Race lies at the center of the UNC story, and few stories offer a more vivid illustration of America's conflicted relationship with race than the one involving sport and the black athlete at Carolina. The story of UNC's scandal opens not on a gridiron or a hardwood floor, however, but in the offices and conference rooms of UNC's College of Arts

---

[12]   https://www.cbssports.com/college-football/news/30-years-later-the-legacy-of-smus-death-penalty-and-six-teams-nearly-hit-with-one/

and Sciences, where the emerging discipline of African and Afro-American studies (AFRI/AFAM) struggled for respect, standing, and resources in the 1980s.

"The curriculum itself started in 1969 during the civil rights era to *redress regrettable intellectual imbalances in the standard curriculum, to help attract more African-American students.*"

Willingham affirms, "The program was not a major, it was not a department. We found a lot of evidence of how many people, both inside and outside of that curriculum, who wanted to be their own department, their own major, and how important that was to those folks at that time." She goes on to say, "The department was not accepted openly from the very beginning. They had to fight so hard for every single thing that they got to be a real curriculum, to be a real department. So they were always the stepchild of the university, always."

According to a timeline[13] published by *The News & Observer* (April 25, 2016) of Raleigh, North Carolina, in 1979, UNC hired Deborah Crowder as the student services manager in what was then the African and Afro-American Studies Curriculum. It wasn't until 1984 that Julius Nyang'oro came to UNC as a visiting assistant professor, tutoring athlete-students for UNC. He joined the faculty in 1990, winning tenure two short years later. In 1992, Nyang'oro became the chairman of the AFRI/AFAM curriculum and promptly allowed Crowder to essentially run the department. She took advantage of her newfound authority and began creating "paper classes" that offered high grades with little regard for the quality of work.

Willingham asserts, "I kept seeing that into the '80s when they wanted to be a major, when they wanted to split off and become a

---

[13] http://www.newsobserver.com/sports/college/acc/unc/article73760402.html#storylink=cpy, Sources: UNC-Chapel Hill, NCAA, UNC Board of Governors, The News & Observer reporting

real department and get scholarly credits, they were still struggling. And I always wondered if Debbie Crowder and Julius Nyang'oro just wanted enrollments, which was another reason to enroll all the athletes, because it would make it seem like there were more students enrolled, and therefore give them credibility. More power to be that strong curriculum and that strong major. We couldn't prove that, but I think we were looking to see if we could prove that somehow."

Moving forward according to the timeline, in 2006-2007, John Blanchard, a senior associate athletic director, and Robert Mercer, director of the athletes' tutoring program, appeared before the Faculty Committee on Athletics and were asked to look into possible independent studies abuse in the wake of a scandal at Auburn University. Both Blanchard and Mercer claimed to have brought up the AFAM independent studies, but other AFAM professors were adamant that didn't happen. Nevertheless, both men were aware that lecture-style classes were being taught as independent studies.

In September 2009, Crowder retired from the university, but in the weeks before her retirement, academic counselors for the football team told players to submit papers to her before she retired so they could benefit from her liberal grading scheme. They later succeeded in persuading Nyang'oro to offer a few paper classes.

Just a few months later, academic counselors for the football team gave a presentation to then-coach Butch Davis and others about the loss of the easy no-show classes, and how this could impact the GPAs of football players. Davis stated that he had no recollection of the presentation.

The original curriculum was actually still being taught, but as the years went by, with Crowder and Nyang'oro leading the AFRI/ AFAM department, the major corruption began.

Willingham said, "In the late '80s, after the deregulation of television, college sports got bigger and bigger and of course the UNC program was also getting bigger and bigger. We had Michael Jordan in 1986. At the same time, Carolina started to become a competitive institution to get into. So you had these two opposites. You had 'we're going to be a sports program, a really strong college sports program,' especially basketball, but probably football too, but 'we're also going to be highly competitive, we're going to only teach to kids who can really score high.'

"And let's be honest, white privileged kids from the prep schools, right? So that's the kind of university we're going to be. So what do we do with these athletes? There's nothing for them. So the harder it gets for regular students, the stronger the admission standards are, the more difficult it's going to be when we let these athletes in. Where are we going to put them? With that dilemma the strong educational classes and the study skills kind of classes started to go away.

"We can trace the system back to 1988; that's when we saw the first basketball players in the AFRI/AFAM paper classes. We think it was then that Burgess McSwain, one of the architects of the paper class system in AFRI/AFAM, and Debbie Crowder started talking, 'What the heck do we do with these kids?' And Michael Jordan, who was a geography major, took a lot of geography paper classes. And Burgess McSwain was in that geography department. McSwain was friends with a gentleman by the name of Professor Birdsall. And together, with Debbie Crowder, they put the AFRI/AFAM program together. A place to house the underprepared athlete. A way to keep them eligible. So it was very intentionally created for athlete-students. These women thought they were really being helpful. They never saw that that's a paternalistic sort of, 'I'm going to help you so that you can play a sport,' but not, 'Let's not give them access to a real education.'"

Willingham and Smith maintain, "Throughout the 1990s athletes went to classes (at least in courses scheduled as regular lecture courses). They showed up and sat right beside nonathlete students who used the courses as genuine learning experiences. On occasion an athlete might even contribute to a class discussion, but, says [Adam] Seipp, a course participant from 1996-1998, 'It was pretty clear they weren't doing the work. We all accepted that. For some reason, we all just accepted that.'"[14]

Willingham and Smith go on to say, "Nyang'oro and Crowder seemed to exhibit genuine sympathy for the athlete-students, and a conviction that athletes 'deserved' the help—not realizing, perhaps, that they only compounded the deleterious effects of an institutional racism disguised by the nonstop celebration of athletic success."

Sonny Vaccaro, a former sports marketing executive, who is probably best known for his tenure with Nike, signed Michael Jordan to his first sneaker deal. Vaccaro says he first noticed that "things" were happening during the years he was involved with the shoe companies and all the NCAA events he helped sponsor in basketball. "As I went through corporate, and I went through the financials of the NCAA, the athletes were the only ones who were getting the worst end of the stick on what was happening as the industry progressed. I'd been on record since 1982. The first time I actually voiced it was on a nationally syndicated television show on CBS, *The Machine*. I've been advocating for a long time, and obviously everything is slow to mature, and it's sort of come to a head. It took a long time to do it, not only from me, but from others, to take a stand against a very popular, fraudulent institution: Amateurism."

---

[14] Excerpt from Cheated by Jay Smith and Mary Willingham.

Vaccaro continues, "The only thing that has been constant are the athletes, and the only thing that's been consistent is the schools being supported by outside entities in corporate America, whether they be the soft drinks, the shoe industry, the phone companies. And they [corporate America] were the ultimate sponsor, giving the ability to the schools to continue on in what they wanted to do for their particular university or athletic department. Whereas the athletes responded with, 'What a wonderful thing.' The universities were like, 'We're going to show your picture all over the world, and thank you.' But not even really a thank you, but 'we're going to use you and sell you.' I think athlete-students are the most overused and abused individuals because others are gaining from them much more than hypothetically an education or even free will. So that is where my crisis started. With the financial end of it.

"Everyone knew about the cheating in classes but the athlete is the one who bears the scar. You're remembered as the guy who didn't take the test. You're remembered as the guy who took the money from a booster. The athlete is an individual, and more often than not, that individual is scorned and their life is thrown apart, and because of whatever 'label' was on him, we all forgot very easily that the schools go on, the coaches go on, the games go on, but the kids are sidelined as a cheater.

"All the kids who had great intentions, who were recruited and induced to go to a particular school, were the ones the coaches were going to take in their gym and show them their names on the wall. Or, go into the football stadiums and see their pictures and all the different athletic situations. It's interesting to me that they induce and entice, and almost promise you that that's going to be you up there on the wall, that's going to be you getting the job, that's going to be you in the NFL or NBA. And truth be told a few choice athletes *will* end up on the top of the heap, their picture *will* be on the way. That's nice. I'm happy for that individual. Good for him. What I'm not happy for are the ones who remain on the virtually anonymous academic pile. The ones who weren't given free choice of their academics. When they graduated they didn't get an education, they got a degree. Or they were forced out; they're always the ones who have no option about leaving."[15]

Universities say, but you're not playing for free. We're giving you an education. Vaccaro states, "I think the term 'student-athlete' makes everybody uneasy. And that starts the problem that's existed since the 1970s. They, being the NCAA, manufactured a term that over the years has totally taken up the mind and soul of the audience, and the manufacturers of this insidious plot, because a student is not just an athlete. A student is a singular thing, and there's not another term where student-chemist or student- musician is ever used, and there's not another term where the student and the amateurism conflict to such a degree that is so biased and prejudiced. The NCAA designed the system to impose these terms on the athlete, when neither the athlete nor the participants, nor the fans, the schools, nor the commercial entities, were even aware anything was going on."

The 2014 *O'Bannon v. NCAA* verdict stated, "the NCAA violated antitrust law by prohibiting athletes from profiting from their names and images in TV broadcasts and video games." It also ruled that universities should be permitted to place as much as five thousand dollars into a trust for each athlete per year of eligibility. The NCAA appealed the ruling.[16] Ed O'Bannon, the former UCLA basketball player and lead plaintiff in the class action suit, had this to say about the verdict: "It was great that Judge [Claudia] Wilken decided in our favor. I think it was an extremely significant step towards college athletes getting paid and controlling their

---

[15]   Based on personal interview with Sonny Vaccaro.
[16]   https://www.nytimes.com/2015/03/18/sports/ncaa-appeal-of-ruling-in-obannon-case-is-heard.html

likeness, owning their own likeness. In that respect the ruling was significant because it was a strong move in the right direction. It was nice going to court and battling with the NCAA, telling them to their face that they need to make some changes to their system. The ruling was the start of really good changes that are still to come about. Now, everyone is starting to see that we need change to the NCAA system. Changes that the athletes deserve. It is their civil right to own their likeness. Everyone else in the world does. Why not athletes?"

O'Bannon continues, "I think the fact that college athletes don't own their likeness is an absolute crime. I wouldn't dare tell the FBI who to investigate, but, honestly, I don't understand why they're not investigating the NCAA today because the NCAA takes these student-athletes' likenesses and sells them long after their eligibility is up."[17]

Michael Hausfeld, one of the country's top civil litigators and attorney for the O'Bannon case, says, "There was an almost century-long tradition of nobody challenging the NCAA's integrity over student-athletes. It was a matter, when brought to our attention, that was an egregious situation, violating many legal principles. Among which were the anti-trust laws as well as just general equity. So making the challenge was important to both address and hopefully correct that injustice."[18]

Sonny Vaccaro, former Nike marketing executive, is candid about the overt agenda when it comes to college sports reform.

The following are Vaccaro's 2001 comments before the Knight Commission on College Athletics, which was seeking to reform the issues in college sports: "I'm not hiding. We want to put our materials on the bodies of your athletes, and the best way to do

---

[17] Personal interview with Ed O'Bannon.
[18] Personal interview with Michael Hausfeld.

that is buy your school. Or buy your coach. You sold your souls, and you're going to continue selling them."

Taylor Branch, an American author and historian, wrote in *The Atlantic*):[19]

> "For all the outrage, the real scandal is not that students are getting illegally paid or recruited, it's that two of the noble principles on which the NCAA justifies its existence – 'amateurism' and the 'student-athlete' – are cynical hoaxes, legalistic confections propagated by the universities so they can exploit the skills and fame of young athletes. The tragedy at the heart of college sports is not that some college athletes are getting paid, but that more of them are not."

The real injustice is that college and pro sports depend on raw material, and that raw material is black muscle. Just like Africans were taken from their villages and sold to slave owners to work their fields, young black athletes are now "harvested" from their neighborhoods and put to work on a football field or on the basketball court. That's the underlying indignity that demands an answer. I concur that athletes agree in essence to participate in their sport; nobody twists their arm to play the game at higher levels. What I have a problem with is the *way* they're harvested, the seeds of lies they're told about their futures, and the fertilizer of deceit and fraud that permeates the whole deal.

---

[19] https://www.theatlantic.com/magazine/archive/2011/10/the-shame-of-college-sports/308643/

2

I was a kid with a talent. That talent involved being a quick learner. I could see an example and turn it into immediate action, yet I never learned my lesson that clashing with the system gets you nowhere. That's why it feels like I'm stranded on an island like Tom Hanks in *Cast Away*, searching for a sign of rescue, hoping someone will see that I am still alive, full of vigor and ambition.

Spending time on an island is meant for reflecting on your experiences. My reflection is that of a twelve-year-old boy who dreamt of becoming the next LeBron James or Kevin Durant.

Without a clue of what lies ahead, blinded by the glory of false advertisement and submissive rewards like shoes, fancy cars, expensive clothes, and big houses, kids are being sold a dream. But they are often jolted awake as adult athletes, in the middle of their own reflection, peering from the outside in, wondering what happened to their soul. Many former athletes will come forth after this book is published and strongly disagree with it based on their own personal experiences, stating that they are happy where they are in life. Yet they fail to realize their loyalty to the *system* has created an illusion that the money and things they have are more than enough. That their experience alone can never be replaced by what has been given to them. They will say publicly that they owe all they have to the *system*, and, secretly, that same *system* says we owe it all to them. The sad thing is that the *system* is laughing at those same athletes.

While at UNC, I often spoke my mind without hesitation. I considered myself the modern-day Nat Turner, leading the rebellion. Naturally, I had my outspoken moments during practices, where I was in disagreement with what the coach saw as discipline tactics. Whereas others were viewed as coachable and compliant, I was seen as uncoachable and disobedient. I was the Kunta Kinte of our team. Constantly running away from the plantation. Refusing to say the new name given to me. Coach Williams would scream at me, telling me to set up a screen or dive on a ball, and I would reply, "Coach, why are you speaking to me like that? You are not my father; my father doesn't speak to me that way." These outspoken moments resulted in running sprints. There were times when Coach would yell and scream and I would not reply at all—I'd just stare at him with a blank look. And he would make us all run because of my look.

I never had issues with any coach until I got to college; I was always a respectful player. High school players get a reputation for being catered to and babied, from schoolwork to athletics. But once it's time to whip you into shape and get you to understand you are no longer in control, that's where the issues start.

It is the coaches, the grown men, who refuse to communicate with the athlete, to teach him, to coach him. But those players who clash are very few and far between, somewhere in the range of one in every five thousand. If you are an avid sports fan, you will hear the media and commentators point these players out right away. I remember an instance during my junior year when facing my collegiate foe, Mr. Julius Hodge. I proceeded to destroy him on our home floor after being robbed of Player of the Year honors the previous year. After a drive to the basket, creating the foul and the bucket, I walked towards our bench looking in the family section at my friends, while giving the throat-slashing gesture as if Hodge was dead meat. I was the best at these types of gestures after baskets—it was a symbol of my swagger, my passion, my game. We went on to win the game. Once I got back to the apartment, my cousin, who attended North Carolina Central and always recorded all my games, was waiting for me to watch the game that my team had just won.

I learned quickly that commentators like Billy Packer, Dick Vitale, and Doris Burke were not fans of mine. During the commentary, Dick spoke boldly as if he knew me as a player and proceeded to throw jabs at my character for making the throat-slashing gesture in regards to Julius Hodge. He continued making comments that I was having trouble with the coaching staff and that my behavior was uncontrollable.

I wondered where he would get such information, since he had never met me. Billy Packer suggested I be "tamed and controlled" because my gestures had no place in the game of basketball. He spoke confidently about my attitude problems and issues with my teammates, yet I didn't even know what Billy Packer looked like.

On the same note, I had spent some time with a young Duke player who seemed to be clashing with Duke head basketball coach, Mike Krzyzewski, more commonly known as Coach K. The player didn't understand why they were clashing; he felt like he was doing everything right and that there wasn't a particular event that led to the problems with the coach. This player said that he had spoken with Coach K many times and he would get the same response: *You're doing everything I want you to do, son. Keep up the good work.*

Months after one particular college season began, I wondered why the Duke player wasn't receiving any playing time. Lo and behold, the commentator cleared up everything for me in much the same manner that I had experienced. Dick Vitale suggested that this player had attitude problems, issues adjusting to Coach

K's system, and that he was a bit selfish. I couldn't believe it. If you were a fan at the time and you heard the comments, you would automatically assume they were true because they came from Vitale. I believe these false statements from commentators still exist, but will never be addressed due to loyalty and submission exhibited by players to the *system.*

***

I was branded as a player who just didn't get it. I could almost hear the remarks: McCants has to have a chemical imbalance or something because he just doesn't care at all about the consequence of his actions, for saying the things that he does. He is the best player we have ever seen, yet he just doesn't get it. Let's send him to the psychologist and see if he can fix him. I saw one psychologist two different times during my tenure at UNC. Two different coaches had sent me to get "psychologically examined."

Granted, I knew how to get under my coaches' skin without being disrespectful. I knew that certain coaches like Roy Williams and Matt Doherty always wanted to be in control and take all the credit. It was when the coach had to take the blame that gave me the greatest pleasure because the situation is always the opposite when it comes to sports: the players take the blame for the loss and the coach gets the credit for the win.

There was an instance when we played the number one team in the country during my sophomore season. I had an opportunity to take control of the game and get all the credit for winning the game. It was a tie game with 30.6 seconds left on the clock. Thirty seconds before that, I'd hit a three-pointer to tie the game and Ben Gordon had missed the go-ahead layup. Coach would draw up a last-second play we had been working on in practice every day during preseason that would give me the last shot. Each and every day of those practices, when I received the ball for the last shot, I made it. We all knew who was going to get the ball. I had prepared for this moment during my entire childhood, when I was pretending to be Michael Jordan.

This was my moment.

We entered the ball at the opposite end of the court. We planned to take some time off the clock, so we ran a play called "freelance" that allowed us to just roam around, passing the ball back and forth until there were about thirteen seconds on the clock. At that point, we got the ball back into Raymond Felton's hands and the play began.

Raymond started on the left side of the floor, as if he were going to get a double screen from Sean May and me, whereas Melvin Scott, who was standing on the left side block, would sprint out the opposite side as if he were coming off a down screen for a three-pointer. Melvin would be the decoy and David Noel would be the decoy screener for Melvin. All the while, after Sean and I set a fake ball screen for Raymond, it allowed our defenders to relax because the ball was going to the opposite side of the floor. We had run this play so many times, we knew it would work. So, after the fake screen, I walked my man down below the free throw line and came off sprinting to the three-point line waiting for the pass from Raymond. I set my feet, received the ball, spread my fingers and flipped my wrist the same way Kyle Lee Watson did in one of my favorite movies, Above the Rim. As I replay that moment in my mind, it moves in the slowest of motions. Lights flashing, crowd cheering, doubt, confidence, reputation, dreams, history. This was my best imitation of Michael Jordan. As the ball rushed through the rim to crash into the net, the crowd erupted. And, naturally, I was the hero. But after the game, Don Markus, a reporter for The Baltimore Sun, collected quotes from Coach Williams and myself:[20]

> Williams: "He made a big-time basket. I think that was fitting for him."
>
> McCants: "It was a dream situation. I never really thought it would happen. Guys like Michael Jordan and Kobe Bryant hit game-winning shots. I always said that if I was put in that situation, I would try to shine."
>
> Markus reports, "But if you listened to Roy Williams, it wasn't McCants who took over yesterday."
>
> Williams: "I don't think he took over. He ran the plays I told him to run. He hit the shots I told him to hit. I think I took over. But he did make a big-time shot."
>
> The conclusion: Slave masters never allow their slaves to outshine them.

***

Being the best player came with the harshest responsibility, and that was to withstand the deepest lashes. I took lashes for teammates that would have broken if hit. I took them for the team over and over again because I was the best player. It's a penalty of leadership, as leadership is not a position or title, but an action and an example. When your best player clashes with the coach, it is the biggest war between two powers. But there is only one outcome, which is victory for the coach, because it is he who has all the troops rallied with him. The same principle applied to Nat Turner. One modern-day Nat Turner is Colin Kaepernick, the former San Francisco 49er, who, on August 14, 2017, started a revolution by

---

[20]   *The Sun* staff, January 18, 2004

kneeling during the national anthem, thereby taking a stand against racial injustice and police brutality. When it was finally noticed after two games that Kaepernick was kneeling during the national anthem, he was asked why. He responded to the NFL by saying, "I'm not going to stand up to show pride in a flag for a country who oppresses black people and people of color." Kaepernick told the media he was kneeling to give a voice to people who didn't have one. A few short months later, the entire nation watched as various athletes, band members, and cheerleading teams joined Kaepernick's one solitary action by kneeling, many raising a fist in the air in unity. One man + one protest = one revolution.

Divisive. Scorned. Vilified. Locked out. Blackballed. One simple, silent gesture sparked a movement toward social justice and racial equality that will forever label Kaepernick as a Nat Turner who was bold enough to blaze a trail for change.

***

Now, let's get back to how the athletic system begins, and who's behind it all.

What's Your Number and What Does It Mean?

How do we place a number on this body of ours? As kids, there is a bidding war for our bodies. Programs like YMCA, YWCA, Pop Warner, Boys Club of America, gymnastics, Biddy Basketball, and even gang organizations serve as recreational streams. But for the more talented youth, they are, as author William C. Rhoden describes, in *Forty Million Dollar Slaves*,[21] "refined pools of talent."

The bidding war starts with the parents. Any parent who goes beyond just allowing his or her kid to have fun playing sports is

---

21 William C. Rhoden. Forty Million Dollar Slaves, New York: Three Rivers Press, 2006.

doing it with financial gain in mind. There is a major benefit for parents to see their son or daughter succeed in sports. They get to live vicariously through their kids in the form of parental guidance, and the child often becomes an extension of the parent's talent or a replacement for a parent who had no athletic talent. The parents are informed that if the kid plays for a traveling team, he can gain more exposure, which could lead to sponsorship and affiliation. Once on a traveling team or AAU circuit, a shoe company that endorses and sponsors the AAU or traveling team is now affiliated with the kid. Gifts range from T-shirts and sneakers to shorts and equipment, and much more that is given to the kids.

Athletes begin to gain a fan base starting in high school as AAU all-stars traveling from tournament to tournament, while recruiters and suitors are heavily pursuing the best prospects. The public sets expectations on us long before we even know what those expectations are; those very expectations will end up being the end-all be-all of your future beyond sports. A successful, high-profile athlete always has a bright future in commentating or reporting for the sport in which they so heavily served in college.

William C. Rhoden writes, "Life on the [Conveyor] Belt often fosters dependency. Star athletes who are so inclined become accustomed to being shepherded through the system without ever having to look out for themselves, from simple perks like not having to stand in line to more serious crutches like being guided through school by tutors and structured study halls."

It didn't cost me anything to play on my traveling team, and every time we went to tournaments, we had new Nike shoes, gym bags, and jumpsuits. At the ages of twelve and thirteen, anything free and Nike meant that you were definitely an elite-level athlete. Kids often exhibit early stages of sports fever as sports creates an idol to pursue, and athletics often becomes that *one thing* every parent is afraid to disrupt in their kid's life: it's called a *Dream*.

Ultimately, parents don't disrupt the *Dream* because the kids become very passionate about achieving that *Dream*. The *Dream* includes the parents escaping poverty and obtaining a better life. College athletics is the stepping-stone to that better life.

I can't imagine a scenario where parents willingly send their kids off to college with the intention of being exploited and wholly used for financial gain. College for all athletes is an honorable accomplishment in sports culture and in American society. Parents are well aware of the financial potential that their kid possesses when it comes to making it to the professional level. Many parents push their kids to the maximum, even when they don't display the talent necessary to make it to the next level. The hopeful thought of achieving the *Athletic American Dream* is a big part of every athlete's ambition.

The circuit of talented athletic machines has surfaced to become the most profitable system in recent history-a farm system of incompetent servants for financial gain. Kids practice every day to become the athletes they idolize without realizing that the athletes they idolize are mere puppets within the *system*, and those athletes are afraid to tell kids the underlining truth of what that fear is, and why the fear exists. The truth is that, on every level of major professional sports, there are overseers and owners that control your every move with rules and regulations. Every sport has a major league, and every major league has an owner or committee that controls that sport. The unspoken truth surrounding sports is that you have a boss, but you will never *be* the boss. You take orders; you will never *give* orders without the capacity to be overruled.

An example of an athlete who did it his way, while his bosses reaped the benefits of his hard work, was Allen Iverson. All Allen ever wanted to do was play ball and win while doing it. He wanted to be himself, dress the way he wanted, talk the way he wanted, play the game the way he wanted, and eventually walk away from the game the way he wanted. Allen thought the game had that much freedom within it, but he was in for a rude awakening when he started receiving a negative reputation around the league for his rebellious persona.

After clashing with his NBA coach, Hall of Famer Larry Brown (who just so happened to be a UNC alum and assistant coach in 1965–1967), Allen saw that the "do it my way" fight was a very hard one to fight alone. As he was traded from the 76ers after ten years, Allen quickly found out that no one was safe in the NBA. Shortly after he was traded, the NBA implemented a dress code that some say was directed at Allen and his hip-hop swagger. But as Allen refused to conform, it pushed him further and further away from anyone giving him favor.

After bringing in hundreds of millions of dollars in marketing ads and sales for the NBA as a star player who merged hip hop and basketball, Allen was left out to dry, not only by the company he promoted, but by his peers. Looking back, Allen would be the first to blame himself, but the reality is, why should *he* have to change to continue creating change?

Likewise, during the 1960s, Hall of Fame basketball star Oscar Robertson took a stance for what he believed. Robertson wrote in *The Big O: My Life, My Times, My Game*:[22]

> "No owner was going to have on his team an outspoken black man making political statements. You can't compare this to modern-day players who refuse to step forward and take political stances because they are afraid of losing endorsement money from a soda company. The

---

[22] http://onlyagame.wbur.org/2011/02/26/big-o

fact is, back then, if you stepped forward and spoke out, your livelihood was cancelled."

This is the underlining truth that athletes face. Isn't it ugly? And to think this is coming from Oscar Robertson, one of the NBA's best players of all time.

The system comes with its own buck-breaking process through coaching and rewards. The reward system is the backbone of submission. The underlying mantra is: *We will give you pennies and the hope of reaching your dream for your hard work in building **our** empire*. Every athlete lives with the fear of losing everything he has worked for. This is a major reason for the submission. The athlete believes that he's being given an opportunity to become more than he could ever imagine along with a standard of living he has only dreamed about.

Dr. Marcus Bright, a political commentator, scholar, and the executive director of Education for a Better America, wrote an article entitled, "Some Black Employees Toil in Sunken Place University,"[23] in which he sheds light on the 2017 hit movie *Get Out*. The movie is about a mind-control process that conditions black people to accept a marginalized status, where they continually choose to go into the backdoors of life. Dr. Bright writes, "The movie was essentially about the 'owners' wanting the bodies and the physical abilities of black men but they also wanted to control their minds. They wanted to control their minds, their functions, and their abilities; so that is reminiscent of high-profit athletics. The system says we want to control…we pretty much want to use your body to make us money for sports. Use your body to entertain the student body. We don't necessarily want you to be a

---

[23]   http://diverseeducation.com/article/94201/

critical thinker. We don't necessarily want you to be successful in other areas. We want to limit your civil engagement to that which is safe…for us. The movie is saying, let's do all we can to control their minds and if any of them step out of line, we'll use the little kettle and spoon to hypnotize them to bring them back into the sunken place. If somebody takes a picture of them and gives them some kind of consciousness, then the guys in charge will make sure to bring them back into the sunken place."

Dr. Bright states:

> The mentality of consistently accepting a second-class placement permeates many universities, and particularly big-time college athletics. Black athlete-students are looked at as a commodity. Any form of militancy, most forms of independent thinking when it comes to social issues and social justice, is strongly discouraged. The system is designed to produce a very docile, nonthreatening, disconnected athlete. A lot of athlete-students come from underfunded, under-resourced school systems so they are more likely to be less academically prepared. The system really tries to control this specimen. Control the athlete and their movements. Control their entire schedule because they're either going to be practicing, at study hall, or in a class. So the university really tries to limit discretionary time and sequester the athlete-student from the rest of the campus a lot of times. The university doesn't want athlete-students getting involved in student activities, per se. Ironically, athlete-students do get a free education, they do get national exposure in big-time programs, yet everyone else is getting paid tangible money but them. You see Alabama football coach Nick Saban making almost ten million

dollars a year on the backs of athletes who are going out and risking life and limb on the football field in pursuit of pro contracts. But with football especially, the kids have to stay in school at least three years. There's really a mind control process. Physically they are able to go out and play ball but their minds are conditioned to really only be concerned about individual advancement and less about uplifting the community they came from and less about utilizing their platform to speak about social issues and social justice. That's the last thing the powers-that-be want.[24]

Dr. Bright is obviously attuned to the *system*, how it works, and how it marginalizes the minds of young athlete-students, predominately black athlete-students. His words reinforce what I'm telling you about the dream, and the illusion that athlete-students embrace.

In the next chapter, we're going to look at what that dream looks like and how it works to marginalize black athlete-students.

---

[24]   Personal interview with Dr. Marcus Bright.

3

The life story of someone coming from nothing and making it to *something* is the African-American dream. The fear of not accomplishing his dream has enabled the athlete to be one-track-minded in regards to his own future and well-being in America. The dream has proven to become a reality for a small percentage of athletes who make it to the pros. But for the higher percentage of those who don't make it, they are forced to window-shop from the television set and think about what could have been if they'd just had a little bit more talent or shook just a few more hands.

***

Leaving the U.S. to play for another country is a viable option for high school athletes. Take Brandon Jennings, for example: after spending his senior year at Oak Hill Academy in Virginia near the North Carolina border, his test scores to attend Arizona did not meet NCAA requirements. So, he was forced to either sit out a whole year and train, or go overseas and compete at a pro level for a year, then become eligible for the NBA draft. Although the option made sense for Jennings, his comments on that option hit home for those athletes who have had academic challenges trying to enter a major university. The following are Jennings' comments on basketball player Aquille Carr:[25]

> "I feel his supporting cast will be the most important thing. Whoever is behind him, who's taking care of his business, that's the most important. If I didn't have my mom and my brother I would have been back in (December). Without them I wouldn't have been able to make it."

In 2005, then NBA Commissioner David Stern[26] created a provision in the Collective Bargaining Agreement simply called "Article X." The provision proclaimed that prospects could enter the NBA Draft only after they were nineteen years old or a full calendar year removed from high school graduation. This one-and-done rule was flagrantly unfair to players who were not only physically prepared to play at the highest level, but who had nothing to gain, and everything to lose, by attending college. While the new rule had its advantages, it did not serve the athlete. Instead, it served the NBA, the university, and the NCAA. Here's how a talented athlete coming out of high school helps the university gain big-time dollars. When LeBron James escaped the college ranks, as did Amar'e Stoudemire, Dwight Howard, Kobe Bryant, Kevin Garnett, and many more, the NCAA missed out on major marketing dollars, alongside gaining affiliation with potential Hall of Fame players.

Putting an age restriction on the NBA forced players to enter into a one-year contract with a university so that they could build

---

[25] Carr played for the American Basketball Association, NBA Development League, and Amateur Athletic Union team.

[26] http://bleacherreport.com/articles/1723163-why-the-nbas-one-and-done-rule-is-causing-more-harm-than-good

a fan base that would follow them right into the NBA. Imagine a player like Kevin Durant, who was prepared for the NBA out of high school, but who was forced to attend the University of Texas because of the rule change. The hype behind Kevin increased ESPN viewers, fans in every city Kevin played in, and sponsorship/advertisement dollars from corporations, shoe companies, and so on. Imagine how many students enrolled at the University of Texas once Kevin showcased his talent. Imagine the recruits who wanted to attend the same university as the famous Kevin Durant. Normally, the high-profile players who leave high school for one year at a university on their way to the NBA are vastly publicized by the media.

Millions of dollars are made in just one year by the NCAA, the university, and the city and state of that university.

Universities pull in twelve billion dollars per year in sports-related revenues on:

- Ticket sales
- Donations
- TV contracts
- Corporate sponsorships
- Royalties from licensing and merchandise

According to Tom Gerencer, head writer at the lifestyle and finance site, MoneyNation.com "How Much Money Does the NCAA Make?" [March 22, 2016], the figure of one billion dollars is often thrown around when describing the size of college sports as an industry. But that one billion dollars is just the NCAA's cut. By far the biggest chunk of college athletics money is taken in by the schools. For all college athletics combined, the NCAA estimates that its member schools make about six billion dollars from ticket sales and merchandise sales to regular-season games. They also rake in an eye-popping five billion dollars from "student fees associated with school athletic programs." With all the uproar over rising tuition costs, an argument could be made that universities are balancing their sports budgets on the backs of students. All in all, college sports is *not* just a billion-dollar industry. Adding NCAA money to school ticket money and student athletic fee money, it's a 12.4-billion-dollar industry.[27]

The moment Durant is drafted into the NBA, there is an exchange of value; Durant's value is in his influence to get fans in the seats and to get viewers glued to the television. This scenario increases the value of the NBA during negotiations with media companies like NBC, ABC, ESPN, TNT, and others. High school players with only regional coverage make it harder to get fans to buy into their first two or three years after entering the NBA. Even players like Kobe Bryant, Kevin Garnett, and Amar'e Stoudemire had to build a fan base with hype they had collected in high school. With the new rule implemented, players would enter the NBA with a following and fan base regardless of which team drafted them.

It is a win-win situation for the NBA and the NCAA.

The NCAA gets one year with America's top-valued prospects with an amazing Return on Investment (ROI) and the NBA gets a prospect with market value and proven results for demographic influence. This is what the million-dollar body does for the invisible empires.

In football, it's even worse, since players must have three years of NCAA eligibility before entering the NFL. This conundrum serves as the largest form of exploitation, since the risk of injury is so much higher in football than in basketball. Andy Schwarz, a California-based antitrust economist, says he envisions a world

---

[27]   http://moneynation.com/how-much-money-does-the-ncaa-make/

in which the NCAA stops worrying about money as a sin, and instead focuses on academic fraud as the more serious issue: "Not to protect the athletes who are hired by schools to provide services in exchange for education but by ensuring they receive the education compensation they receive."

Schwarz adds, "The biggest impediment is that the NCAA does not see itself as a protector of athletes' rights to an education but rather as a sort of Owners Union protecting the sports product sold by schools and serving to cartelize wages."[28]

Collegiate baseball doesn't have a rule for how long you have to stay in college before entering the majors and there are no rules exempting athletes who go to the major leagues straight out of high school. I wonder why. Is it because less than 5 percent of African-American baseball players come out of major universities? Is it because baseball isn't as attractive a sport for African-Americans compared to football and basketball?

Obviously, you'll have your own answers. The NCAA and universities prepare million-dollar bodies years before the culmination of big bucks on the field or court. The various levels of the farm system consider black athletes an investment of potential profit. High school prospects are given a ranking number according to their potential ROI.

The AAU circuit and traveling teams give the athlete visibility for comparison with other athletes. From year to year, the system allows for basketball and football coaches and scouts to rank athletes by position based upon ability, availability, flexibility, personality, and other traits. The university is making the investment in the athlete-student by providing a scholarship, but make no mistake, they are investing in our talent, not our ability to get an education. In return, athletes make the universities billions of

---

[28] Personal interview with Andy Schwarz.

dollars that they are not sharing with the athlete—much as the purchase and sale of slaves.

A slave owner would buy the slave at x amount of dollars, and in return the slave would help the slave owner make x amount of dollars, and all the owner had to do was give the slave a place to sleep and food to eat. Looking back at my years playing ball, and observing the houses my coaches lived in, it's laughable to think that the coaches actually cared about the athletes, despite what they knew about their living conditions and upbringing.

Former NFL defensive back Anthony Prior, author of *The Slave Side of Sunday*,[29] said in an interview with *The Nation*: "Black players have created a billion-dollar market but have no voice in the industry, no power. That sounds an awful lot like slavery to me. On plantations slaves were respected for their physical skills but were given no respect as thinking beings. On the football field, we are treated as what appears like gods, but in fact this is just the 'show and tell' of the management for their spectators. In reality, what is transpiring is that black athletes are being treated with disrespect and degradation. As soon as we take off that uniform, behind the dressing room doors, we are less than human. We are bought and sold. Traded and drafted, like our ancestors, and the public views this as a sport, ironically the same attitude as people had in the slavery era."[30]

The money made at UNC-Chapel Hill while I was there, and after the basketball team helped the university become the campus it is today, with new buildings, facilities, and much more, was made possible by the sweat and hard work of athletes who got nothing in return. And when I say nothing, I'm including the fraudulent education that was given as a distraction to keep

---

[29] https://www.thenation.com/article/slaves-game-adrian-peterson-and-s-word/

[30] January 20, 2006.

our mouths shut. Look at my sixteen teammates, who said they received a great experience and great education at UNC.

I would ask those guys, "How does a predominately fraudulent education compare with the billions of dollars in profit that you made for the school?"

These sixteen guys say they would much rather have experience and education, which they all currently don't use as a part of their careers, than a piece of the billions of dollars made off their backs. I must be the craziest athlete on this planet to see the injustice. At least the coach will invite them to the annual fish fry every year. I, on the other hand, will be eating Chipotle on that day. As Joseph Forte, a former UNC basketball player, attests, "Getting a quality education as an athlete, especially a star athlete, is like getting the Walmart version of education, not the Nordstrom brand."[31]

The education plantation process continues with the university investing in the prospect, giving him a scholarship that includes room and board and occasional food. We received one meal card, which allowed three credits per day. Breakfast, lunch, and dinner. If we missed any of those meals, we wouldn't eat until the next one was available. And if we missed dinner, too bad. In return, the athletes promise (in writing) to not make, take, or facilitate any money on their own, and not break any rules that have been enforced upon them. This system results in the athlete serving the university as a top-notch athlete and serving the classroom as a subpar student.

It is assumed by the university that if you are an athlete, you are more focused on making it to the pros than gaining an actual education, even though athletics is in itself a form of education, albeit not book learning (except the playbook). Sports has its own education system that requires studying and constant prepara-

---

[31]   Personal interview with Joseph Forte.

tion in order to be successful. Regular (nonathlete) students don't have to worry about double homework and writing a paper while getting up at 5 a.m. to train and run sprints, shower, make it to breakfast, and then be on time for English 100, all the while trying to process the playbook for practice at 3 p.m. so they have an opportunity to break into the lineup for the game on Friday. After all, when you're an athlete, your family will be there and you want them to see you play, not benchwarming on the sidelines.

Sonny Vaccaro has this to say about the stark difference between "regular" students and "athlete" students: "In reality, when a regular student enters into a university, he has an option of choosing his curriculum, picking the times when he goes to school, and even picking his classes and teachers; he has free will to do whatever, and the student (or his parents) are paying. That student might also be given a scholarship for expertise in another area. Maybe it's an academic scholarship. Maybe it's the Goodwill scholarship. Maybe it's the Lion's Club scholarship. Other students get scholarships also, but they're never preempted by an athletic department or a specific team rearranging their academic life. That's been constant. Conversely, an athlete can be a good student and go to classes, and try to do the work, but because of the rigorous training that goes into a high-level athletic program, the time and the essence of one's life for a twenty-four-hour period doesn't allow the athlete to get what the other students are getting. So I'm saying it is fixed in the sense that the academic world has sold their soul to the athletic world for the betterment of the university's finances."

Willingham and Smith agree: "There is a widespread belief [at UNC], as at many universities, that it is acceptable to hand black athletes counterfeit educational credentials since real credentials will lie forever beyond their grasp. At least they were given the 'opportunity' to spend time on a college campus, goes the thinking. (Self-satisfied and privilege whites tend to chalk up classroom shortcomings among black athletes to laziness, lack of drive, and 'cultural' issues.) These attitudes are insulting, offensive, and destructive, but the fact that they simmer just beneath the surface of polite university discourse helps explain both the institutional refusal to take AFRI/AFAM seriously and the long-term toleration of the department head's solicitous caretaking of athletes and other students (many but not all of whom were black…The [AFRI-AFAM] department was regarded by some as a *cargo bay* for students who somehow had to be 'cranked through' the system…only the numbers mattered; quality control was completely ignored."

The term *cargo bay* reminds me of the slave ships that housed slaves as they were being transported from Africa to America. Tight pack. Loose pack. Just get them in there and keep them alive. Numbers. Money. Labor. Not that much has changed.

Since the 1900s, when universities were established and sports teams started to assemble, the only reason athletes became students was for financial benefits—that is, benefits for everyone but the athlete. Back then, sports betting was very prominent and one aspect of that profit sharing was to charge fans to come see college athletes play a professional sport. Ultimately, athletes were admitted to a university just to play sports and help the university make money. It was the social benefit of sports.

There has been no reform except for some fancy words and a contract called the National Letter of Intent, which I'll address in Chapter 6. It's no secret that American schools are under-performing in comparison to other schools around the world. The American school system is a success at the Ivy League level because those are the schools that breed American leaders. The other schools breed entertainers, and we all know that entertainers don't need to be smart to run and jump, right? But the truth is, athlete-entertainers *do* need to be smart to calculate plays and understand schemes and strategies. Yet when those same athletes come to the end of their sports career, they are disregarded as useless baggage to American society.

College for athletes exists merely for sports, but to be fair, there are a few who take full advantage of their academic experience while gaining promise outside of sports. Those athletes tend to be players who aren't as athletically gifted as in the profit sports of football and basketball. If your ROI isn't as high as the star players' you *must* have something to fall back on, and your education will most likely provide that fallback. Some athletes are conscious of these realities and act accordingly, while others keep their eyes on the prize of pro sports.

Mary Willingham reveals, "HBO did a piece that I was in, and they actually tested a kid who was still at the middle school [academic] level, but he was a football player who got a college degree. So I mean, it's all just monkey business from the standpoint of everybody is just playing games to keep these kids eligible and to maybe give them some sort of degree. I think if somebody's already pretty strong, if they've taken a lot of AP classes in high school, they've had a lot of access to tutors, and they go to school year-round, I think getting a decent education is possible, maybe even exceptional, but definitely not the norm. The academically gifted and talented kids could probably do it. The NCAA loves to show their propaganda machine for those kinds of cases. But it's just very unusual. We as white privileged people in charge of all these institutions truly believe that we are giving black athlete-students a chance that they wouldn't otherwise have, right? So the Admissions Director would say, 'Well, if we didn't have them here, where would they be?' Like they're better off here. It's almost like we're playing God with these kids' lives. And it's like our values and our judgments are on somebody else's children.

"I feel so strongly that it's not about playing king for the day and deciding what our kids should get. It's about asking them what it is they want. It's like all the kids that I worked with had real hopes and dreams for a better life for themselves and a better life for their family. And we decided that we were going to take those dreams away from them because we put them in a major that wasn't going to be helpful to them or their family, if they even do graduate. We don't pay them, when we should at least pay them for work study for all the hours they put in as undergraduates representing the university. It's just another system in this country where we – and I put myself in the category, because I'm also a white, privileged person – decide what's good for poor people, and we make those decisions without them even being at the table, without even asking them what it is they want. In a way, sometimes it feels hopeless. Because I want it to change but I don't know that I'm going to see it in my lifetime. I have a lot of faith that Rashad and his constituents, and the children who are in college right now, are not going to tolerate these unjust systems. Because they see it for what it is[32]."

Before I attended boarding school in New Hampshire, I was a student at Clyde A. Erwin High School in Asheville, North Carolina, where I was a subpar student receiving the same dismal grades that other star athletes receive. I often sat in the back and slept in class. I acted as the class clown for the first two years of high school and maintained a 1.8-2.0 GPA doing absolutely nothing. It seemed okay to misbehave because no one ever complained to me or my parents. Of course, my parents were disappointed when I brought my report card home and showed it to my father. I got mainly Cs and Ds, which led him to remind me of the type of man I would end up becoming if I didn't take my schoolwork seriously. My father always told me to look at the guys I was playing

---

[32] Personal interview with Mary Willingham.

against at the park. He would tell me, "*Picture yourself twenty years from now on the corner selling drugs because you didn't take advantage of your opportunity.*" He told me in his "father voice" that basketball wouldn't last forever, so I must prepare for life after basketball, and he always ended with the fact that education was important for my after-sports life.

When I made the decision to attend New Hampton School (in New Hampshire), it was solely for academics. I was good enough during my sophomore year to receive a scholarship from Clemson University. I was ready to accept the offer that very moment, just because I didn't think it would ever happen. But my father said, "There is a lot more where that came from, son." Once I got to school in New Hampshire, I took everything more seriously; I was on a mission to prove to my father that I could be smart, that I could be anything I wanted to be. And after two years at New Hampton, I received Student of the Year two years in a row. My GPA improved from a 1.8 to a 3.3 and I was able to get into any college I wanted.

Nothing was handed to me at New Hampton. Teachers and staff paid attention, as there were smaller classes and attention to all details, with study halls and tutors. It was a blessing to experience what college felt like before I set foot on a college campus. This is how I knew I was at UNC for sports, and sports alone: UNC didn't match the high school academic experience to which I had grown accustomed. There were to be more revelations about the tactics that universities employ to engage the athlete-student in their system.

One of those tactics is where the "dream" is sold to the athlete during home visits and phone conversations. First, coaches in nicely pressed slacks and crisp shirts convey what a great academic experience you'll have, promising that they'll return you better than when you arrived. Then the university virtually tells you, "We are giving you a first-class education in return for your athletic abilities, hard work, and dedication." The NCAA chimes in with their slogan *interpretation*, which is: *Free Education, No Compensation.* The message is very clear that they are laughing in our faces as we continue to make them hundreds of billions of dollars year after year without any questions or concerns. A decade later, I realized how much money was being made in relation to how much education was being offered, and what I found was a disturbingly defective form of slavery. The term *indentured servitude* continued to pop up when revisiting my college experience. I was working for free, promoting a product in which I had no stake.

Then there was the lie. Education is supposed to be given to athlete-students in return for their hard work and dedication. It is a "reinvestment," which, once the sports life is over, gives that athlete a shot to live the American dream. That fact takes us back to the number placed upon the athlete as a symbol of his value. The athlete's body can be worth millions of dollars, but once the brain is valued at ten cents, statistics show that the athlete is likely to end up right back where he came from."

Billy Hawkins, professor in the Department of Health and Human Performance at the University of Houston, says, "When universities detach athlete-students from the educational process through paper classes and fraudulent grades, one of the major issues it causes is an increase of disdain and disconnect from what it means to be properly educated, or the learning process of acquiring knowledge at a university: the classroom discussions, the debate, the challenging of ideas, etc. Another issue is the further isolation and alienation this creates for athletes. The system that's in place encourages academic fraud."[33]

---

[33]   Personal interview with Billy Hawkins, Ph.D.

The stats tell the story:

> Professional teams hold 1,696 total player spots every year in the NFL, 440 player spots in the NBA, and 224 player spots in the MLB. Among these three sports, there are 2,360 athlete millionaires with million-dollar bodies. Yet there are thousands upon thousands of athletes who don't make it to the professional level and are left to retrace steps to the place where they started. It all starts within the educational system and society's system, systems that have been in place for hundreds of years.

From kindergarten through twelfth grade, the family unit is no longer needed; obedience and conformity is instilled in children through social/educational interactions with authority figures who are not their parents. Therefore, the school system can identify which child will be a great citizen through obedience and conformity, by way of statistics and grading scales of biased and strategic information. Dr. Marcus Bright says, "There is an issue of academic preparedness that links down to the K-12 school system in terms of athletes coming in to universities and not being academically prepared. Academic preparedness is more to the fact that they are producing inordinate sums of money for the educational institutions yet the families in large part come from poverty, living in trailers, living in very tough conditions."[34]

To illustrate my point, I refer to Michelle Alexander's brilliantly-written, yet disturbingly factual book, *The New Jim Crow: Mass Incarceration in the Age of Colorblindness,*[35] where she talks about the *school-to-prison pipeline.* Her basic premise is that the educa-

---

[34] Personal interview with Dr. Marcus Bright.

[35] http://www.newjimcrow.com

tion system is set up to fail young African-Americans, so they're directed into the incarceration system, which works as an ongoing cash cow for the government.

The *school-to-prison pipeline* is designed for athletes who don't necessarily have the potential to be stars. If you can't read at a third-grade level by the fifth grade, your name is placed on a list and passed on throughout the prison system. The list means that prison beds will be built in penitentiaries for those kids who are on that list. The pipeline creates a perception that if you're in school and you can't read, we know you're going to break the law. We know you're going to be rebellious about things you don't understand, because you can neither read nor write. So the chances of you becoming a felon or a criminal are higher than it is of you becoming a normal citizen because of your education. So the athletes who can't read at a third-grade level can escape the clutches of prison by shooting a jump shot, running a route, or hitting a pitch.

The Netflix documentary *13th* supports my point by taking an in-depth view of our economic history of slavery and the post-Civil War discriminatory legislation and practices that replaced it with "systems of racial control" and "forced labor." The film explores how, for many decades, the demonization of underserved and underprivileged minorities has added to the unrealistic fear of minorities by whites. Those athlete-students who don't cut the muster on the field, court or in the classroom are virtually doomed from the start.

You go into the school system with hopes and dreams, and all your attention directed toward becoming a great athlete, and in the midst of all the activity you forget about your education. Then comes the day when you're not good enough to make it to the next level, so the only life left is the life in your home environment. The reality is starker for the African-American athlete. If you don't have potential to be a sports star, your only option is to survive in whatever other environment you find yourself in; but, remember, within that environment, you have to take into account your education. If you cannot read and write at a third-grade level, and you are a teenager, the chances of you becoming a criminal or being arrested are significantly higher than winning the lottery or making it to the pros.

The background, environment, and upbringing of any young athlete make buying into the "lottery ticket" dream even more alluring: you know you need the opportunity to work out because there is nothing else on which to fall back. There's the young African-American guy of who lives in poverty and who needs to get his family out. The sentiment is, man, I just want to make sure my mom gets out of the 'hood. I want to make sure we get out of the ghetto. There are a lot of black athletes who came from nothing. Their whole dream and promise to their family goes like this: *I'm going to make it to the NBA and be rich one day and get you out of here.*

And that's the whole lottery ticket fantasy...the dream. Are you starting to get it?

The truth is: If you don't have a wicked jump shot, you're going to be selling rocks. Either you're going to excel in sports, or you're going to excel in being a criminal. One or the other. As a result, the pressure on a kid in the ghetto to become successful in a profit sport is enormous. To that point, Dr. Marcus Bright says, "I think the big question is, what happened to all the other black males and students in general that went to Rashad McCants' middle school and high school who didn't make it to the NBA? What was their level of academic preparedness? What life opportunities did they have? Were they recruited to colleges? I think that's a bigger part of the systemic issues. I'm much concerned with the millions of other young black males who didn't make it to North Carolina or other learning institutions. And the fact that these institutions only value black men for what they can do on a basketball court or football field. The only time young black men are celebrated or valued or appreciated is on the athletic field. That's what incentivizes them. They aren't pursued in other arenas, or supported."[36]

***

Without sports, our society has already prepared the fate for those with a ten-cent brain. The people in the *system* know that if you can't read and comprehend the laws of our great nation, then the only place for you is in prison. African-Americans comprise 13 percent of this country's population and yet make up 40 percent of its prison population.

Nationally, according to the 2010 U.S. Census,[37] blacks are incarcerated five times more than whites are, and Hispanics are nearly twice as likely to be incarcerated as whites.

Race/Ethnicity	% of U.S. population	% of U.S. incarcerated population	National incarceration rate (per 100,000)
White (non-Hispanic)	64%	39%	450 per 100,000
Hispanic	16%	19%	831 per 100,000
Black	13%	40%	2,306 per 100,000

This is no coincidence. There is a *system* in place and the *system* is one of absolute corruption.

If we are a race that has no future beyond the fifth grade, imagine the pressure for those who have no idea they are participating

---

36   Personal interview with Dr. Marcus Bright.
37   https://www.prisonpolicy.org/reports/rates.html

in a *system* designed for their failure. It is abundantly evident that I have surpassed the expectations society has placed on me. I have avoided prison, made millions of dollars, built self-sustaining businesses, and decided to give my life experience to the next generation of African-American youth.

The biggest question to date is where do we go from sports? Prison? Back home? Drug dealing? Coaching? Training? When you're done with sports, or when sports are done with you, the moment you attempt to live as a common man, your denial or acceptance depends on your being under- or overqualified for the position. As an athlete-student at a prominent university, you would think that affiliation alone would grant you an opportunity to be "all that you can be." But the term "dumb jock" didn't spring out of nowhere; it's a stereotype that excludes athlete-students with hopes of becoming more than just an athlete in today's society. Joseph Forte acknowledges that, in his post-school life, he benefited from the prestige and reputation of the name UNC However, the education he received was a nonfactor. He admits he learned a few things in drama class about messages in movies, nonverbal communication, human interaction, and learning how to read people, but his education did not translate into business acumen, or anything else, for that matter. Forte states that the university "communicated clearly to me that I was there for basketball." He says, "College was simply an extension of high-level basketball camp…that's it. I liken it to psychological, systematic buck-breaking."

Forte continues, "When I played in the pro arena, coaches and management played tricky games off the court to keep their slaves in order; if you don't submit to their power, they will marginalize you, label you as nominal. It's very covert…they do a good job of making the player look like he's crazy. Players comply out of fear of trauma. Terror of getting PTSD. There's always an underlying message to the slaves: Do what they say. Don't become unruly."

I believe that two forms of exploitation continue in America: The exploitation of college athletes and the exploitation of entertainers within the entertainment system. I have been subjected firsthand to such misperceptions while residing in Los Angeles. Attempting to take my innovative ideas of social media and music development to big companies, I was immediately categorized as an ambitious athlete with no knowledge of the business. I was always introduced as Rashad McCants, the NBA player who had played at UNC. On one hand, that celebrity benefited me as the face of a product, or as a promotional tool with my reach and access to other players and celebrities. On the other hand, it undermined me as a human being, a professional businessman. Our expectations of athletes are just that, an expectation of an *athlete* and not a citizen, or human being. We *are* the entertainment. African-American entertainers since the 1800s were not meant to be smart, knowledgeable, or intelligent, only obedient and submissive. The ruling class of America is filled with nonathletic figures of bloodlined ancestry, and this new billion-dollar system of servants surprisingly revolutionizes slavery as a free will, reward-based entitlement.

Forte agrees. "The 'masters' are looking for a certain kind of young black male: no dad in house, economically depressed, because they are more easily 'trained' to submit. UNC seemed to feel obligated to expose the shortcomings and weaknesses of those who spoke out like Rashad and myself. It's a betrayal of trust by UNC. But Rashad has moved past the label placed upon him, yet the label itself gives him a platform. It's such a travesty that young athletes are told they're going to get a *free* education. The cloak of deceit has to be unveiled that the university has one reality for the student and one for the athlete. Plowing the fields for talented young athletes is the ultimate plantation education in the way they go about choosing the educational path for the athlete-student[38]."

I made my fair share of a few million dollars, more money than many will ever see in their lifetime. Yet now that I see the *system* and how, without African-American athletes with million-dollar bodies and ten-cent brains, there would not be a billion-dollar market for sports. Nonetheless, if we all came together and used our ten-cent brains in unison, we could configure a billion-dollar business and a first-class educational institution, but it appears that it's just a dream. Martin Luther King, Jr. was murdered for his dream, his vision of a future, a future with promise and great potential. One day, we will have our businesses and institutions, and one day we will look back and see that it all started somewhere: with one voice that proclaimed an elaborate plan for something much bigger than anything the common man could comprehend.

A plan of revolution, a plan of destiny, a plan of righteousness for those who will never understand how we could go from having nothing to gaining everything.

---

[38]   Personal interview with Joseph Forte.

4

On numerous occasions throughout my sports career, I have been labeled unfathomable names. I have been referred to as bipolar, enigmatic, mercurial, psychotic, problem child, bad teammate, and uncoachable, just to name a few. My father always raised me to be true to myself and told me that I owed "no one nothing."

Speaking my mind has always been therapeutic, but during most of my sports career, I held back so much that I wanted to say, things that I should have said much earlier. I, too, suffered from the reward syndrome of submission knowing that sports were the only outlet to escape the clutches of the ghetto.

I grew up in Asheville, North Carolina. We lived on section 8 housing, which is a housing program that offers affordable housing choices for very low-income households. We often received government funding for food and living. My mother was a hair stylist and my father was an ex-war vet working as a machinist. Although life was tough financially, my parents always made us feel like we had more than the average poor kid, so coming home wasn't like living in a rat hole or a place we couldn't tolerate. Our apartment was very lavish and upscale, filled with a big screen TV, cable, a nice leather couch, and sound system with fifteen-inch speakers; it appeared we had it made if you were looking in from the outside.

No one ever knew it was all rented, but it didn't matter; we had no shame.

My dad's brothers were football stars who were much younger than him. One of his brothers was just a few years older than I was and I often got to hang out with him. John Avery was the first out of our family to make it to the NFL from college. He went to the University of Mississippi as a running back and he was the best running back I had ever seen in person. I consider him better than Barry Sanders, but that's just me.

My dad's other brother, Petie Scarbourgh, attempted to go to junior college, but his grades became a hindrance. Petie was a wide receiver. Petie's talent was my motivation to become the third person from our family to make an impact in the sports world. John had made it to the NFL and now I had an opportunity to make it to the pros. I was a clear shoo-in to make it to the NBA after the age of twelve, as I started to grow and gain major exposure on the AAU circuit, although I was never seen or looked at as the savior of my family. My sister, Rashanda, who was two years younger, also had basketball promise, alongside my first cousin, Cameron Maybin, who is currently an MLB star for the Miami Marlins. Our family is full of talented athletes! I honestly think we all have the same mentality when it comes to playing our sport, and that is to show the next generation that anything is possible if you set your mind to it.

***

For many years after UNC, I was loved by fans for the rare entertainment qualities I possessed: mixing passion, charisma, and the determination to win. But while I was at UNC, I was deeply resented by the athletic department. I could feel the negative energy every day when I entered the basketball office to begin my daily workouts. After a while, I would only go to the gym at night to avoid the negative energy. It was a huge burden as I struggled to figure out where I had gone wrong. There was a banner in the rafters, my jersey alongside it; I had accomplished the very feat I had set out to accomplish when agreeing to attend this university. I thought, how is it that these people can't appreciate the time and work that I've supplied for them to reap monetary benefit and fame? After ten years, I figured it all out. As a representative of UNC, my comments and state of mind affected their future revenue streams.

Even my tattoos became a reason for some people to consider me somewhat crazy. After all, what kid would brand himself with the words "Born to be hated, dying to be loved?" The AFAM classes taught me that American society viewed Africans as an abomination to the land. There was so much hatred and pain in every story about Africans becoming Americans during the more than four hundred years of slavery. It is as if we as a race are all born to be hated, despised, mistreated, unappreciated, and made to feel like *less than*. And until the day of our death, we continue to seek love, appreciation, acceptance, and the understanding that we are more than men…we are gods and kings.

My tattoos helped keep those thoughts in the back of my mind—the notion that I always had to prove myself. I always had to prove I wasn't who they thought I was; I was so much more than an athlete with a skill set. And ten years later, as I look at my tattoos, they only make me smile with such joy to see how far I've come. I see that my life's work will be more than a memory, more than a basketball game, and more than a jersey, but a symbol of power, freedom, and righteousness. I can understand when my tattoos are misinterpreted as crazy or "out there" because, at the end of the day, my non-conformist tattoos are the one thing that separates me from everyone else.

The figures before me were guys like Phil Ford, Michael Jordan, James Worthy, Sam Perkins, Vince Carter, Antawn Jamison, Jerry Stackhouse, Rasheed Wallace, Kenny Smith, Rick Fox, and Hubert Davis, just to name a few. All these sports figures were men of great accomplishments, yet each held their university to the highest standard for both education and athletics. So when one "bad apple" emerges from the group of legendary players, this bad apple must be the crazy one. How could the bad apple speak against the one place where all these great players came from, without one complaint from any of them?

Maybe it's because my million-dollar body didn't pan out in the NBA the way I envisioned it. Or maybe my ten-cent brain didn't fight through all the adversity to reach my goals the way the public had envisioned I should.

***

Mary Willingham personally observed many athletes at UNC who could not read at a third-grade level, yet were high-profile athletes destined for the professional level. With that in mind, the sole purpose of a paper class is to make sure that the athlete-students who *do* slip through the admissions department and make it to campus receive special treatment to keep them eligible, rather than making an effort to educate them. The university doesn't have teachers who teach fourth-grade material for college students, which is why a woman as brave as Mary Willingham stepped forward, as she continuously discovered many kids who just could not do the work, or even comprehend the simplistic reading assignments given to them.

Willingham says, "No one at Carolina was ever allowed to say anything bad. That's like a part of the culture there, so when I spoke out about these athletes who were underprepared, I was called a racist. I was told by the Chancellor that I was actually marginalizing students and that I was creating an uncomfortable situation, and how could I ever say such a thing as a teacher? But as a teacher, and especially a reading teacher and a learning specialist, if I don't know what level my kids are at, I can't really help them. Shoving them into college-level classes if they can't read the material or do the work, that's not helping them. So that's always my point. But nobody at Carolina—I mean, they pretended like they didn't understand, but I think they just don't want to understand."

When asked if it's remotely possible for an athlete to get a solid education in a legitimate major when the demands of practice and performance are the primary aspect of their university life, Mary answers a resounding no! She explains, "Some people would look at an athlete-student who couldn't read at all and say, 'Hey, now he's in medical school.' And that's just a lot of hogwash. The problem is, it's not that you can't learn to read at any age, but your vocabulary is so deficient that you would really struggle. You'd need a lot of development or remedial work to catch up. So we've just been passing you along all these years. And half of the players don't get a college degree anyways. Half of the Division I college athletes, I mean the statistics are out there, but I would argue that the half that do are either kids who have had access, or kids who are just getting passed through.

"So we'd have to take a look to see how many of those degrees are legitimate, and what level readers the kids are at the point that they have a college degree. Their GPAs are pretty low, so it's not like they go to graduate school, and that's what I would always say about African-American Studies was: what do you exactly do with an undergraduate degree in African-American Studies? If that's really your choice, you probably go to graduate school, right? Because you'd want to study and research, and perhaps you want to teach it. I know for a fact that you would find zero athletes who followed up and went to school to continue their education. Because they couldn't."

With what Mary is saying, we cannot ask the question of how these kids got here when they can't even read because the answer is in front of our eyes: the coaches walked into their houses and sold them on a great athletic experience with the hopes of making it to the NBA or NFL. It's a fact that no college coach can promise an excellent academic experience.

Dr. Marcus Bright asserts, "The priority in many cases is for athlete-students to stay eligible as opposed to trying to actually learn or gain tangible skills and credentials that will make them viable in today's job market. A lot of the more lucrative jobs are going to be in engineering and computer science. These higher-demand courses are largely discouraged for athletes in favor of less rigorous majors in terms of just trying to keep them eligible. That means that for many of those who don't make the league, their likelihood of being viable in the economic market is significantly reduced. I went to school on a basketball scholarship and I think athletics is wonderful but when you invest everything in it and there's not an academic incentive, it can be problematic."[39]

Professor Jay Smith has a lot to say about Roy Williams's knowledge of paper classes:

> "When Roy Williams came here from Kansas, he brought with him the team academic counselor who had served him so well at Kansas: Wayne Walden…He [Williams] regarded Walden as such a vital contributor to the good fortunes of his teams that he was practically moved to tears when Walden departed in 2009. Walden knew every detail about the academic lives of those

---

[39] Personal interview with Dr. Marcus Bright.

players; he had to. He registered them for their courses, for crying out loud. [And that means he got on the phone with the Department of African and Afro-American Studies and he put them in paper classes.] Walden also spoke with Williams every day; he had to. Williams' claim that he had no earthly idea that his players were floating along on paper classes – and that he never would have guessed that one of his stars was enrolled in four no-show classes in the spring of 2005 – is nothing more than a confidence trick. He's counting on the customary journalistic favoritism, and journalists' amazing lack of curiosity, to enable him to tell this whopper and walk away with his aura intact. We'll see if that works."[40]

Roy Williams had a few choice comments of his own: "I strongly disagree with what Rashad (McCants) has said. In no way did I know about or do anything close to what he says, and I think the players whom I have coached over the years will agree with me. I have spent 63 years on this earth trying to do things the right way and the picture he portrays is not fair to the university or me."[41]

In another interview, Williams asserted, "I don't have control over the academic side. But the academic side and our athletic director and our president want me to emphasize the academic side every single day, and they want our players to understand that…They want us to be concerned and to emphasize it but they

---

[40]   http://sports.yahoo.com/news/unc-professor-blasts-university-and-its-athletic-heroes-in-defense-of-rashad-mccants-164401647.html

[41]   http://www.usatoday.com/story/sports/ncaab/2014/06/06/north-carolina-roy-williams-rashad-mccants/10065937/

don't want us to step over to the academic side. They don't want that to happen."[42]

In light of some of his comments, it seems that Coach Williams doesn't, in fact, have control over what classes the athlete takes or doesn't take. But I find all that irrelevant seeing that the coaches don't get their checks from being academic instructors; they're athletic coaches. And although there are many passionate coaches in America who would coach for free, virtually none would pull up to the arena in a brand-new BMW 745 and thousand-dollar suit. I don't think the high-dollar coaches would give up their salaries just so a kid could feel like he was getting a great education. This is still America and if it isn't about the money, what is it about?

What I am telling you is not a personal attack on coaches; rather, it is an attack on the ten-cent brain, where the athlete makes the mistake, not the university. Where the athlete is at fault, not the coaches or administrators. It is the dumb jock athlete who decides to take easy classes to stay eligible, and continues to make millions of dollars for his coach and university, in return for a piece of paper that says he has been validated to participate in society.

Congratulations, you've reached and exceeded ten-cent-brain status.

---

[42] http://espn.go.com/espn/otl/story/_/id/11047963/north-carolina-coach-roy-williams-disbelief-rashad-mccants-claims-academic-fraud

5

My sixteen teammates from the 2005 championship team signed a statement that said: "With conviction each one of us is proud to say we attended class and did our own academic work." It's public knowledge that at least five of my teammates who signed the statement, who went public to discredit me, actually took more than ten paper classes. Not only is that fraud, it's lying to the public and defaming me.

The truth is clear: You did it to protect the plantation. Again, it's that Willie Lynch mentality I talked about in Chapter 1. Protect the house at all costs.

So when Coach Williams approached players with, "Hey guys, I need you to sign this paper that proclaims you didn't have the same experience as Rashad," they looked at each other as if to say, "Do we really want to go against Rashad? Because Rashad is a cold-blooded motherfucker. We don't want to go up against the other guys but we still want to come around campus and we still want to come to the games and be cheered when we're at the games. We want people to cheer for our names and have something positive to say about us. So we're going to roll with Coach on this one."

***

Debbie Crowder was our advisor for AFRI/AFAM and we had to turn in papers to her. Any time a class changed direction, or we needed to take special summer courses, we went to her. She was basically like our sub-advisor when it came to what courses we wanted, taking us out of courses, putting us in courses. Debbie was simply part of the system as a whole. Everything was already set up the way they wanted to do it. Go to this class. Go to that class. Make sure everything is seamless for the athlete-students. Joseph Forte remembers, "When I got to UNC I wanted to be a business major; they persuaded me not to take that major. They strongly urged me to take core courses, which were not beneficial toward obtaining any degree. They made it clear that I was there for the basketball program. My focus was to be on basketball. I don't recall taking any paper classes; I attended classes and enjoyed my academic experience. Tutors were aware of athletes' schedules but they didn't write papers for me specifically. They do hammer it into your brain though—you are not here for school, you're here for basketball."

Dr. Nyang'oro was the Swahili instructor, so when we needed to take a language, a lot of athletes took Swahili because it was an easy A. I personally took Swahili I and II and actually learned a little Swahili. Although we had to sit in the classes, we had cheat sheets for all the tests. Our advisors gave us the actual tests because they already knew what he was going to give out.

***

How It All Starts
The AAU Farm System

The Amateur Athletic Union (AAU) was founded in 1888 to serve a number of amateur sports. Today, there are more than 1.1

million AAU members, but nearly 50 percent are for basketball. In 1978, Congress passed the Amateur Sports Act, which had a huge impact on how the AAU would operate. Under the act, a national governing body was set up for each Olympic sport, which basically removed the AAU from those powers. The AAU then refocused its efforts largely on youth sports, which is still the case today.[43] The AAU was created for a pipeline to Little League Baseball, basketball, soccer, and a host of other youth sports.[44] AAU athletics implemented a ranking system that allowed high schools and colleges to predetermine who would be a five-star, four-star, or three-star athlete.

In this farm system, you start a kid off in third grade, and by the time he is in high school, recruiters know how good the kid is because he's been ranked since a young age. These recruiters are not attached to the universities. They are third-party contractors that scout younger talent who can be prepared for the high school level and then for the college level. As third graders progress toward fifth grade, recruiters get a ranking of the top one hundred athletes in the region, and then nationally. In each major city, recruiters are watching kids play and ranking them in the top hundred in that state. Just like adults are given Social Security numbers. The numbering system provides a way to identify rising athletic talent, and the young athlete moves up in the system as he gets older.

As you go from fifth grade into eighth grade, as a player, you are knowledgeable about your ranking, and you're trying to get as high as you can, because the goal is to get to the NBA, the NFL, or the MLB. The family pressure, and the mental pressure of performing, is strenuous, but the farm system only gets bigger as the talent that succeeds at the higher level becomes even more success-

---

[43] https://www.active.com/basketball/articles/the-history-of-aau-basketball?page=1

[44] http://www.aausports.org/_

ful. The more success athletes experience on the professional level, the more the farm system expands, and creates more motivation for parents to push their kids towards sports instead of academics. The success level seen on the national scale, whether it be on television, radio, or what have you, is very appealing to family units, yet parents often don't consider that the number assigned to their kids, whether it's good or bad, keeps them in the system.

The athlete-student continues through ninth, tenth, eleventh, and twelfth grades, trying to enhance and increase their ranking. Universities use the ranking system as an investment tool, and ultimately the numbers become more economic than informational. It's what corporate America calls ROI: making the best possible investment and reaping the best possible high-reward scenario. In the farm system pool, the goal is to find athletes who can rank between five-star and four-star, who can bring you the best return on your investment. There's a one hundred thousand dollar to two hundred thousand dollar investment, per player, for four years. And in those four years, for the money the university spends, they're hoping to get a return through that scholarship that they've given that player. The return is based on the ranking of the player, how good he is, and how many people will come see him play. It boils down to how many people you, as a player, can put in the seats. Five-star camps like the Nike camp and the adidas camp exist to showcase the young talent to the universities, so the universities know what type of investment to go after.

In his book *Forty Million Dollar Slaves,* William C. Rhoden writes about the *conveyer belt system*. Rhoden says the book's title "cuts to the chase in describing the white wealth-black labor [coined in Claud Anderson's book *Black Labor, White Wealth*] condition that has merely changed forms from generation to generation." He continues, "Even in 2005, with African-American athletes making up a so-called majority in professional football and basketball…access to power and control has been choked off. The power relationship that had been established on the plantation has not changed, even if the circumstances around it have." Again, we see the Willie Lynch "control your slave" mentality alive and well in universities everywhere.

The AAU system of numbering everything plays into educational quality starting in elementary school. There's a lot of leniency in elementary school athlete preparation because if you play sports in elementary school, the teachers allow you to skate by because of your potential. Depending on the environment, minority kids who live in lower income conditions also have a worse educational environment than others, especially when it comes to basics like reading and writing. Again, it's part of the school-to-prison pipeline. A pipeline that is mired in dirt and controversy.

In a July 20, 2011, article about the apparent suicide of a Houston AAU manager in the midst of Southeastern Conference investigation, *SB Nation* reporter Andrew Sharp wrote, "For a solid 25 years now, AAU basketball has been a cesspool for corruption and deceit and conflicts of interest." There's a hierarchy of power and control within the AAU that continues to define which kid gets what attention and by whom. If you take the private school kid and the public school kid into account, there's much more attention given to the private school kid. Since he has the potential to make it big as a college athlete, he's going to receive lenient treatment because the school knows his focus is on sports. The minority kids with talent are not taken as seriously.

In his book, *Dead Coach Walking: Tom Penders Surviving and Thriving in College Hoops*, Penders, one of the winningest basketball coaches in NCAA history, sharply criticized AAU coaches for their links to sports agents. He called for background checks and barring college coaches from attending AAU-sponsored events. In 2012, AP reported that four AAU summer league teams were banned from participating in the July evaluation events because of ties to sports agent Andy Miller, founder of ASM Sports agency.

Parental pressures and expectations also play into the overall scenario because if parents see their child excelling in a sport, those parents—that single mother, that single father—think their athletically-gifted child is their lottery ticket to escape financial pressure and stress. A lot of families even go into pregnancy with the expectation that they are going to birth the next sports star. So they already have in their mind what they're going to do when the kid is two years old, and how they're going to train him to be the next star. The parental pressures when it comes to sports have everything to do with the potential of being a millionaire. Like I said, it's buying the proverbial lottery ticket…buying your ticket means you've put your kid in the farm system. Everyone has full knowledge they can play the lottery, knowing that you will most likely not win. The same goes with sports. The chances of a youth athlete making it into the pros is two to five percent for every athlete, depending on the sport.

The numbers are all there: one hundred thousand kids in high school are playing sports, and only four thousand are going to go to college. Out of those four thousand, only three hundred are going to the pros, and out of those three hundred, only five are going to stay. What parents don't realize is that forcing potential into their kids to be great, even if they're not great, is bad for business.

Because now the market and the farm system are oversaturated with athletes. It's almost like a "keeping up with the Jones" mentality. A parent can see another parent's kid being successful on the field or the court and say "my kid can do that too," and then force their kid to do something that he doesn't necessarily want to do, simply for bragging rights.

I also believe the reason why more and more parents are so aggressive on the field and in the stands is because there is so much national attention on the younger players now. I've personally worked with a lot of kids training in Los Angeles, and a lot of the parents are so hands-on now, even though they have no experience, because they want the attention that the kid is getting. The parent has pushed his kids to be something *he* wants them to be and has placed his kid in the spotlight that he's always wanted to be in. It's called living vicariously through your kids. But there's another danger that lures young athletes into the vortex of self-deception, and parents have nothing to do with it: it's how the kids view their sports and entertainment idols.

Take some time and look at all the iconic figures; research their history. When it comes to Jay Z, Little Wayne, Denzel Washington, and Will Smith, they did not necessarily excel when it came to education. They excelled through opportunity. Kevin Durant completed one year of college. LeBron James didn't go to college at all, and he's highly successful, almost a billionaire. So the message that's being sent, from my perspective, is that you don't have to go to school to be successful. The message being relayed is focused on sports. No matter what you do, if you focus on sports, you can make it.

So as idols, athletes are given salesmen responsibilities, to sell their propaganda of going into sports. Whether an athlete is promoting Gatorade, Spalding, a tennis shoe, or the NBA, kids are watching and saying, "Wow, I really want to do that. I want to grow up and be like Kevin Durant. I want to grow up and be like this guy or that guy." The immediate impact and message is that kids start thinking they don't have to focus on education, that they don't have to know how to read or write because the athlete is not promoting education—reading, writing, business and economics—or any other important aspects of life. This mentality is essentially hurting the younger generation because the idols and role models are being bought to sell the sport, and *only* the sport.

***

The NCAA empowers the superstar athletes who pedal the idol mentality yet handcuffs the athlete-students once they're involved. Once the net is thrown over an athlete-student, the enslavement begins in the form of rules that most often make no sense whatsoever.

Now, let's look briefly at a few of the absolutely ludicrous rules of the NCAA handbook:

- In 2015, three University of Oklahoma students had to "donate" the cost of the extra pasta they ate to a local charity to safeguard against an NCAA violation.[45]

16.11.1.10 Incidental Benefits—Reasonable Refreshments. An institution may provide student-athletes with reasonable refreshments (that is, soft drinks, snacks) for student-athlete educational and business meetings and, on an occasional basis, for celebratory events (that is, birthdays). [R] (Adopted: 10/28/99)

- On another occasion during the 2013-14 year, the Mississippi State Bulldogs self-reported twenty-one violations, two of which were stickers and an extra table. The Bulldogs host "Junior Day" by sending invitations to football recruits. The school put stickers on the envelopes, which apparently is a no-no according to the NCAA rulebook. They also had a table in the locker room to hold equipment, which under the guidelines constitutes a "special addition," so they had to report it.

---

45   http://mentalfloss.com/article/62221/9-most-absurd-ncaa-violations-recent-memory

- The father of a former Notre Dame football athlete wanted to take his son and a couple of teammates out to eat after a winning game. The coach informed the father that he could only pay for his son's meal and not the meals of the teammates. The father promptly stared down the coach and said, "You mean to tell me that my son's friends (who have no money) have to sit there and watch us eat?" The coach nodded his head affirmatively. The father chose to covertly disobey NCAA code and paid for all the young athletes at the restaurant.
- According to NCAA rules, players who can't afford cell phones cannot make birthday calls to their mothers or anyone else from the coach's office.
- The most preposterous of all was the incident where, in 2014 at the University of South Carolina, a cookie cake that contained extra icing was served to recruits, which constituted an NCAA violation. NCAA rules state the following as a violation: *Impermissible iced decorations on cookie cakes given to prospects.*

According to the documentary *$chooled*,[46] "A mass murderer in the legal system has more rights than a student-athlete in the NCAA system."

The NCAA is a nonprofit organization doling out rules and regulations to young athletes who are working for free while they're getting money, which creates a type of criminal fraud. Statistically, America is one of the worst countries in the world when it comes to education, simply because it's not predicated on building businesses—it exists to create workers, not bosses. The NCAA is selling the dream of *free education-no compensation*, and that's doing noth-

---

[46] https://www.amazon.com/Schooled-College-Sports-Sam-Rockwell/dp/B00GM2MSGY

ing but setting us up to be workers if our sport dream doesn't pan out successfully. It's a form of modern-day slavery, but the design is not just directed at African-Americans—the reconstruction of the design is for everyone. So now what you have is not necessarily a *system* but a dream state, an illusion.

It's this national illusion that says you must go to college and learn twenty-five subjects, and then choose among those twenty-five subjects what you want to do with your life…for the rest of your life. The twenty-five subjects are the only subjects available. So when you're talking about education, you're talking about bosses and slaves. Names from every race have chosen to be a part of this system, and if you are of privilege, if you come from a blood line-privileged family, you can escape being a part of the system simply because you are already a boss. You don't have to go the educational route to own a business because you've already been handed the keys to companies and businesses that you own or control. Blacks, whites, Latinos, everyone, are all programmed to chase the Fortune 500 companies, learning what it takes to be a part of these five hundred companies. Under these five hundred, there might be another one thousand that we are working toward, hoping to get a minimum wage, low-level entry job because there are simply no other options.

When you really think about the system of labor, and system of education, there is no color barrier. Those in power want as many workers as possible. And if you want smart workers, you know you can get the Asian worker; if you want obedient, submissive workers, then you choose the African-American worker; and then you have the Caucasian worker, who is the more efficient worker because he has more information. The information comes generationally, so you understand what you need to do to make better use of the options given to you. That information is not given in the African-American community. Black business ownership is not taught or pushed. It is provided and encouraged in the Asian community, which is why there are Asian businesses set up everywhere. The underlying theme of the entire multicultural system is, "Hey, we want you guys to work. We don't want you guys to own. We don't want you to control. We want you to be controlled."

Gladiators and Emperors

In the movie *Gladiator*, the objective was to fight to the death; fighters only fought others to the death because they wanted to stay alive for their families. The emperors created these spectacles to distract the public from the political laws they were creating. The same thing occurs in sports today. We are the new gladiators. Back then, gladiators were praised. They were praised as gods almost, and the emperors hated that some of the gladiators were praised more than the emperors. The emperors knew that, essentially, the power was in their hands, and the same applies to today's administrators, the NCAA, and NBA and NFL owners.

They are the emperors, and they put on sports shows and events to create a distraction amongst the public to hide how much money is really being generated by the emperors. Think about it. There are thirty teams in the NBA, thirty-two in the NFL, and thirty in the MLB. That makes ninety-two owners, and if I put a number on how much money collectively those owners have, it would blow people's minds. These are people who could possibly control the world, single-handedly: less than one hundred people who are pulling in somewhere in the neighborhood of fifty trillion dollars a year in the sports market. That's why the gladiator never questions, never challenges the emperor...because the gladiator sees the emperor as the power. The gladiator just wants to stay alive. He wants to preserve what little he is being given and not jeopardize what little he has; he wants to keep his family afloat, and just keep steady. I believe this falls in line with indentured servitude, which requires an understanding of one's circumstances.

The circumstance of an indentured servant is that you get room and board; the master takes care of you as long as you take care of the master. So as long as you're doing your duties, you will be fed, clothed, and housed. Any violation of that could result in you being terminated. So indentured servitude does have a lot to do with appreciation of the master. And it has everything to do with appreciation of your circumstances.

When it comes to athlete-students, we get a dorm room, we get three meals, and we get the opportunity to better our lives through the university. That is the only promise we are given. Not the promise of money, not the promise of information; it's simply a lottery ticket. You may make it. You may not. Living as an indentured servant means we're working for free. Although you volunteer to be an indentured servant, when you don't have the proper information to make a good choice, you're definitely going to be willing to become one. That said, when it comes to the university, of course I want to be here because there is a goal in mind. That's exactly what makes me an indentured servant; because they are sharing the goal with me. *Hey, you want to get here? The only way you can get here is to come through here, boy. So come on over here, but look, we're not going to give you anything, although we'll pretend to give you an education.*

The thing is, you never get there. You always stay here. "You can always come back and we'll have open arms for you." That is what every single servant loves about the university. I can always attach myself back to the place that gave me my chance. And that, to me, is the plantation. Every player speaks to the plantation because he knows there's no other place to go. We had no identity, we had no home, we had no nationality, and so what do we do? Hey, this place [university] is not that bad. The slaves know nothing of what it feels like to be the master. Black is a color. White is a color. We're not people. We're people *with* color, but we don't have any representation. So, if black people are being killed in the street, and there's no justice for it, it's because black people don't have any representation. We're just immigrants, violating laws in a land that's not ours, and we seem to be ignorant to how the system works to our demise. There's a certain privilege—they call it white privilege—yet white privilege doesn't even belong to white people. White privilege belongs to all people. I can say that I'm white too because it's just a color. Hear me? It's *just* a color! So, I can say I'm a white man and you can respond, "No, you're not!" But I can retort back, "Yes I am, because I said I am. I want white privilege, so consider me white."

Another aspect that plays into the university experience is the social interaction of sports. Attending a university can give you a social advantage, because you can interact with diverse cultures, which can enhance how you talk, how you walk, how you dress, and the people with whom you choose to hang around. The way you socially interact will help you get a job, or not get a job. If you come from the 'hood, and you're socially incompetent, it's going to be evident immediately, and people are going to shy away from you because you don't have any potential to be socially competent. When you are in circles where proper social interaction is key, your environment and where you came from can be the separation that continues to divide the successful from the unsuccessful.

So where you come from plays a huge part in your overall success, simply because it exists as a divide within social interaction.

2ND QUARTER

The Problem with Plantation Education

Part I

6

The National Letter of Intent

So many athletes with million-dollar bodies and ten-cent brains have been adversely affected by the National Letter of Intent (NLI) program for breaking rules they had no idea even existed up until the moment the offense happened. And at that precise moment, their athletic career is jeopardized for being a rule breaker, a line stepper. I can only imagine how the careers of guys like Terrelle Pryor, Maurice Clarett, Johnny Manziel, Reggie Bush, Cam Newton, Donnie Edwards, Todd Gurley, Jameis Winston, and many more would have turned out if they had not signed the NLI and still went forth with amazing football careers without incurring punishment from the NCAA for not signing the NLI.

Let this be a warning: If you are unable to read and comprehend the message of the NLI contract, then you will forfeit your opportunity to make money. On any account, if an athlete violates a rule set by terms of the contract, that athlete jeopardizes his opportunity to make a better life for himself through sports—the one thing for which he has spent his whole life preparing.

The powers-that-be know that the athlete is so encouraged and happy to be given a shot at his dream that he would never forfeit the opportunity to use the NLI path to reach that goal. Realistically, college is the main route to make it to the million-dollar payouts, and the NCAA and every big-revenue university knows it.

The National Letter of Intent contract is based on the *intent* to exploit you.

There is no direct connection between the NCAA and the athlete before the NLI is signed. You are a regular student who is interested in attending a university. Regular students must submit an application to get accepted by the university. Therefore, the university, the NCAA, or anyone else for that matter cannot tell that student what he can or cannot do. The student is free to make money for himself or herself via work, promotion, and any other legal avenue. Also, the student can receive outside financial aid from any source available to help their living conditions.

The NLI is the third-party program that connects the athlete with the NCAA and the university. As an athlete, you are entering a program in which your university acts as your representative. Also, the NCAA manages this program alongside the CCA (Collegiate Commissioners Association), which provides governance oversight of the program.

According to the NLI website:[47] "The NLI is a *voluntary* [emphasis mine] program with regard to both institutions and athlete-students. No prospective student-athlete or parent is required to sign the National Letter of Intent for a prospective student-athlete to receive athletics aid and participate in intercollegiate athletics, and no institution is required to join the program.

"By signing a National Letter of Intent, a prospective student-athlete agrees to attend the designated college or university for one academic year. Pursuant to the terms of the National Letter of Intent program, participating institutions agree to provide athletics financial aid to the student-athlete, provided he/

---

[47]   http://www.nationalletter.org/aboutTheNli/index.html

she is admitted to the institution and is eligible for financial aid under NCAA rules. An important provision of the National Letter of Intent program is a recruiting prohibition applied after a prospective student-athlete signs a Letter of Intent. This prohibition requires participating institutions to cease recruitment of a prospective student-athlete once a National Letter of Intent is signed with another institution."

The NLI website states:

> The National Letter of Intent has many advantages to both prospective athlete-students and participating educational institutions:
>
> - Once a National Letter of Intent is signed, prospective athlete-students are no longer subject to further recruiting contacts and calls.
> - Student-athletes are assured of an athletics scholarship for a minimum of one full academic year.
> - By emphasizing a commitment to an educational institution, not particular coaches or teams, the program focuses on a prospective athlete-student's educational objectives.

If the NLI is a *voluntary* program and athletes can still receive scholarships and participate in athletics, what is the true purpose behind this program? Why is there a hidden agenda behind the program, where the athlete forfeits his or her ability to make any money at all in college due to hidden rules bound by a fraudulent contract?

Former NBA star and current basketball analyst Charles Barkley confessed on *The Dan Patrick Show* in September 2010 that he broke NCAA rules while playing for Auburn: "I got money from agents when I was in college in the '80s. A bunch of players—most of the players I know borrowed money from agents.

The colleges don't give us anything. If they give us a pair of sneakers, they get in trouble. Why can't an agent lend me some money and I'll pay him back when I graduate? These agents are well, well-known. They've been giving college kids money for thirty years... And I've got no problem with it. I want to visit my family; I want to go see a movie. How in the world can they call it amateur if they pay eleven million dollars to broadcast the NCAA Tournament?"[48]

Lack of Insurance

The biggest problem with you not having insurance is that, as an athlete, you can attend a university, get hurt in your freshman year, and there's no workers' compensation or guarantee you'll be playing again, or anytime soon. You're basically left out to dry, even if you have a bright future: you don't have the money to pay for private insurance and the university is not putting it up for you, so you're pretty much stuck in the wind. Without insurance, if you get hurt, you face a number of problems.

An excellent example of what can happen is also featured in the documentary *$chooled: The Price of College Sports*, which tells the story of Kent Waldrep, an athlete-student at Texas Christian University (TCU), who was paralyzed when he broke his fifth cervical vertebrae after landing on his helmet in a football game against Alabama in 1974. TCU cited that Kent was an athlete-student, thus volunteering in extracurricular activities, which didn't warrant any kind of insurance to pay for his hospital stay, or many surgeries, because he wasn't a *worker*. On the other hand, if we were workers and being contracted to work for the university, we would then be offered workers' compensation and insurance by the university. But since we are students first, and we are volun-

---

[48]   http://www.al.com/sports/index.ssf/2010/09/barkley_admits_he_
        took_money_f.html (Doug Segrest, The Birmingham News, Sept. 21,
        2010)

teering to play in extracurricular activities, there is no insurance or workers' compensation covering us.

Academic Expectations

The academic expectations you enter the university with give way to academic disappointment after your athletic experience is over and you find yourself without a quality education. The previous academic requirement for NCAA Division I schools was sixteen core classes in high school, a 2.0 cumulative grade point average or higher, with a 2.5 GPA, 820 sliding scale on the SAT and graduation from high school. In 2016, the SAT sliding scale remained the same, but two changes passed. First, you must have a 2.3 GPA in core classes. Second, you must complete all ten core classes before your senior year. No longer will there be an opportunity for you to get better grades or recover lost core classes. Most athletes want to be more and do more to further their career outside of their sport yet are unable to focus on their sport as much as they'd like to due to collegiate academic requirements. So there's a double-edged sword when it comes to academic requirements and standards. The athlete-student is there to play sports and provide a service; therefore, they should be contracted as a third party and paid to play any kind of sport at any university that's making money. No questions asked. No academic requirement necessary. After all, the athlete is not there to showcase the university's academic reputation. He's there to showcase the team!

Sonny Vaccaro points out, "There's a famous case in Minnesota, in which George Dohrmann, author of *Play Their Hearts Out: A Coach, His Star Recruit, and the Youth Basketball Machine*, won a Pulitzer Prize for writing a series of stories about the basketball coach at the University of Minnesota who told kids they didn't have to do anything. Every paper was written, and the kids basically didn't have to do any schoolwork. The NCAA investigated the case, the coach was fired, but Minnesota lived on. Athlete-students don't have to go to class. Someone writes your paper. Or they say we'll put you in this class and you'll get a guaranteed 'A.' It goes against the core and integrity of what the school is there for. To give athlete-students an education."[49]

At this point, you might be asking, do *any* athletes get a legitimate education? Is it possible for an athlete to go to all his classes, satisfy all his requirements, and still excel on the field or the court? The answer depends on your view of what education is supposed to look like. If your definition of education is going to class, receiving passing grades, getting a certificate, and not really receiving any specialized knowledge in a career field, then yes, many athletes get an education.

Every day we hear, *you should go get your education.* There's no emphasis on what that education really is, where it leads to in America. What does an education actually mean, by definition, in America, and what does it really get you? How far can you really go with an education when, historically, guys like Henry Ford, Walt Disney, and Napoleon Hill—guys who become millionaires and billionaires off of pure imagination—simply used what's called ambition, passion, perseverance, and pushed to achieve a goal, without having a high school education? It affects not only athletes; it exists within inner-city schools all over the country. It's like we're being filtered through it and we don't question the system. It's just "how it is." It creates the whole worker mind-set of today, which dictates that you don't question who you're working for or why you're working; you just know you have to work.

Internships and Legal Liability of the University

Four-year scholarship scenarios play out as four-year internships. In her *Huffington Post* article, "11 Ways College Athletes Are

---

[49]   Personal interview with Sonny Vaccaro.

Treated Worse Than Unpaid Interns,"[50] Caroline Fairchild states: "Overworked and often discarded after years of constantly putting their bodies at risk of injury, these young men and women are the basis of a sports industry that pulls in billions of dollars. Yet they often can only watch as video-game companies, apparel companies and coaches cart away millions, while their own scholarships can disappear at a moment's notice." Ms. Fairchild points out a multitude of ways in which athlete-students lose out while coaches and merchandisers gain riches galore.

Which laws determine when an intern should or should not be paid?

The Fair Labor Standards Act, or FLSA, regulates minimum wage and overtime for U.S. workers, including interns. The Department of Labor's Wage and Hour Division is responsible for enforcing the law, and has a six-factor test to determine whether interns at private-sector employers must be paid minimum wage.

According to the Department of Labor,[51] an *unpaid* internship must meet *all* of these criteria:

- The internship is similar to training which would be given in an educational environment
- *It's for the benefit of the intern.* (University scholarships are for the benefit of the university, not the athlete-student, especially with the inferior educational standards allowed for those who perform well on the court or field)
- The intern doesn't displace paid employees
- *The employer doesn't benefit from work the intern is doing, "and on occasion its operations may actually be impeded."*

---

[50] https://www.huffingtonpost.com/2013/09/06/college-athletes-un-paid-interns_n_3865911.html; Caroline Fairchild, Huffington Post, Dec. 6, 2013

[51] https://www.dol.gov/whd/regs/compliance/whdfs71.htm

(The university and NCAA both benefit monetarily from the work of the athlete-student)

- *The intern isn't promised a job at the end.* (Unpaid "tryouts" aren't allowed)
- *Both the intern and his/her boss understand it's an unpaid position.* (The only understanding is that the coaches, university, and NCAA profit from the work of the athlete-student with no promise of a future whatsoever)

Professor Maria Ontiveros at the University of San Francisco School of Law, wrote an insightful, intelligent research paper entitled, "NCAA Athletes, Unpaid Interns and the S-Word: Exploring the Rhetorical Impact of the Language of Slavery,"[52] in which she notes, "Though studies and commentaries vary, a general consensus is that student–athletes spend approximately fifty hours each week during the season on their sport. For football players, the season ranges from fourteen to nineteen weeks, most of which is during the school year. For basketball players, '[a]t some schools, the road to the NCAA men's basketball championship may require student-athletes to miss up to a quarter of all class days during their spring semester.' During the off-season, players are often required to attend practices, team meetings, and conditioning. For many athletes, playing a sport requires as much time as a full-time job."

"Everyone gets paid in big-time college athletics except the players, who actually risk their bodies to provide the show. The NCAA dubs them 'student-athletes,' using the claim of 'amateurism' to deprive them of any remuneration. But big-time college sports aren't like the amateur sports of a Division III school. The demands on the players aren't voluntary; they are mandatory and consuming. The injuries they risk aren't minor; they can be career-

---

[52] July 16, 2015

or even life-threatening. It wasn't a good idea for the South to base its economy on slave labor. And it isn't a good idea for universities to be the producers of professionalized, big money sports entertainment. It surely conflicts with the stated educational mission of the university."

Ontiveras quotes author Danielle Lyn:[53] "'What made the thought of human slaves so desirable and accepted? They worked on plantations and produced generous income for the plantation owners at no expense. Basically, they produced money but never acquired compensation for their work, resulting in greater revenue for the plantation. Sound familiar?'"

In the corporate workplace, you can host an intern for a year and then the company can end up hiring that intern if the person performs well and fits into the company's culture. There are two forms of fraud involved with what we consider an internship: the first being that you can't have an internship that lasts longer than six months without actually producing a job opportunity outside of that internship. Participating in an internship does not guarantee a specific outcome; therefore, there should be a guarantee that you'd be offered a job outside that workplace.

The employer applauds and appreciates compliance among his employees and wants you to fit in to the *status quo*. The employer rewards you if your behavior fits in with other employees—conformity is the name of the game. If the employer likes your performance and behavior, management will refer you to more jobs and opportunities; and if they won't, then you won't go anywhere. That's the gist of it, and the reality of it all is that sports and business are pretty similar, just a different playing field, so to speak. If your employer doesn't like you, managers won't refer you to the next level and those people who call for references…well, you'll

---

[53] Danielle Lyn, NCAA: Slavery or Free Play?, http://truegridiron.blogspot.com/

get a bad recommendation. As in an office environment, if the boss doesn't like you, it sucks to be you. In sports, you can still be a high-performing athlete and while that might give you more of an edge, it doesn't guarantee you anything past your playing days. There's no strategy or planning beyond the day you step off the field. There's no discussion, and if anything is going to change for the athlete-student, there needs to be some type of conversation.

Internships in the corporate world require you to sign over the ability to interact with any other employers or competition in the same field. When you sign up for a university internship as an athlete-student, you are forbidden to interact with boosters, agents, or anybody who can offer you anything that could be seen as a threat to the university's existing system. That's basically a noncompete agreement. When you sign a noncompete in your internship, you know you're not being paid, but it's preparing you for the next level that you're trying to reach in your chosen career field. And within that legal stipulation, internships can only last a certain amount of time. And what's more, in sports, if you get hurt, your internship is terminated immediately.

Did you hear me? Immediately!

Within the limited amount of time the athlete-student has to act as an unpaid intern, legal stipulations still exist within the scholarship. You are completely overlooked because it's called a scholarship, and because it has to do with education. So, in terms of the internship, you can be referred to the next level of job experience, depending on how long you stay at the school interning. If you did a one-year internship, your résumé is going to look different than it would if you did four years. Now, if you did a one-year internship at a university, your employer is unhappy that you did only one year. Your employer is going to move on to the next employee because maybe you don't have enough experience to go to the next level. You don't want to be in an internship where you're working for free, and then again, you have to cushion the relationships between employee and employer because the employer has everything to do with your future in that workplace.

In "Modern Day Exploitation" [U.S. News & World Report, April 10, 2014], Susan Milligan starts, "They were called 'breaker boys,' the children who worked long hours at low pay in the mid-19th century through the early 20th century separating impurities from coal on a coal breaker. It was hazardous work, with the boys having their fingers bloodied up or even amputated by the conveyor belts. Some lost feet, arms, hands or legs when caught in the machinery. Others were crushed by the equipment and killed, their bodies noticed only at the end of the work day by supervisors." She likens their plight to college athlete-students: "College athletes are similarly mistreated. They may not look as pathetic and tragic as the breaker boys, but the same dynamic exists: they work long hours, making millions and millions of dollars for the NCAA, the networks, the advertisers and the coaches. But underneath the glamour of being a college basketball or football star is an ugly truth. Most don't end up being drafted into the pros. They get academic scholarships (with barely any time to study), but they are not guaranteed for the four years of school. They do not receive long-term health insurance—a particular problem given the risk of concussions among football players."

Psychological Control over Athletes and Their Dreams

Psychological control goes back to the lottery ticket, which is the first psychological mind-fuck that the athlete goes through. As a kid, you're seeing that dangling carrot in front of your face, but you're not even understanding what that carrot is. You just know it's dangling in front of you and you're looking up at it like, I want it. It's the kind of situation in the beginning where, if three kids are doing it and I'm the only kid who's not, I might as well go over and do the same as those other kids. As time goes on, we see the scenario of selling the propaganda of sneakers: they wear Michael Jordan's, they wear Nike, they wear Tiger.

The system has been in place since Sonny Vaccaro started show deals for college athletes in 1978. Once that happened, there was a perpetuation of understanding of who exactly to pursue to gain influence over the younger audience. You get the best player, you give him the dopest shoes, and everyone is going to go out and buy the shoes. That's the number one profitable item for athletes, tactically, in the business. But outside of that tactic, you gain an amount of influence and build the reputation for this one person who's selling his shoe. He, as the salesman, gains influence on everything he does in his life. Vaccaro explains, "In '76 when I went into the commercial end of it, I saw what I helped create by subsidizing athletic programs with paying coaches, then eventually paying all universities, and the company I represented. But the consistent thing that I saw were the athletes. And if you live as long as I've lived, and you've seen as many kids as I've seen, some of them don't end up with a fair shake, and as time goes on, it starts to get to you."

Now as a social media follower, you're following LeBron James and he's become more than just a shoe salesman: he has a lifestyle, he has character, and he is a role model, somebody the kids want to grow up and be like. So now it goes outside the shoe salesmanship and into social prestige, and when you blend social prestige with commercial salesmanship, you have this unbelievable machine when it comes to young kids and dangling that carrot in front of their faces. Now, there is a generational propaganda that says, you need to play sports, you need to be rich, you need to be famous, you need a Mercedes-Benz, and you need a mansion. And when you need all these things, the only place you need to look to get all these things is the easiest possible route—play sports, because it's the most promoted and propagandized business on the planet.

Unlawful Athlete Protests and Boycotts

In 2015, the state of Missouri[54] came up with a new law that basically states any athlete who protests will lose his athletic scholarship. The last thing any university wants to experience is a protest or boycott by athletes. Period. Unfortunately, the stranglehold in the mentality of the athlete-slave is so strong that the fear of potentially losing everything he waited his whole life for is way stronger than standing up for injustices. As Joseph Forte puts it, "The institutional slavery mentality has to be broken at its core for any lasting changes to be made."[55]

In the Missouri situation, athlete-student Jonathan Butler, member of a campus group called Concerned Student 1950, went on a hunger strike, calling for the resignation of University of Missouri system President Tim Wolfe, citing Wolfe's inability to correct a host of racial injustices on campus. Wolfe ultimately stepped down because he knew full well that money lost in just one game is not recoupable to all the investors. If, on a Saturday or Sunday, fans show up to watch a game, but no players show up to play, you have a bunch of people who paid for tickets, endorsements, advertisements, and then there's what ESPN paid: everyone loses money that day if you do not show up and play. It's similar to a stock market crash.

Now imagine if black people were so mad about the system that not one black player played in a game until the problem was fixed. Talk about making a dent in the system! The real problem is that the systemic, Willie Lynch mentality is so much stronger than any kind of revelation or liberational thought, so that me trying to be the next Malcolm X or Martin Luther King Jr. means nothing

---

[54]   https://www.si.com/college-football/2016/11/08/how-missouri-football-has-changed-1-year-after-boycott# (Nov. 8, 2016)
[55]   Personal interview with Joseph Forte.

compared to the hold the system has on the mentality of the slaves. The system will never be reversed until the proper information is given to African-Americans. For the sake of argument, say that all black athletes boycotted football or basketball games. Without black athletes, you lose the entertainment value. You lose the fanfare. Really, what the NCAA or universities *don't* want is any kind of house nigger, house slave, or field slave to entertain independent thoughts about rebellion because they know what the ramifications will be—financial ruin.

Ed O'Bannon cites the following reasons why college athlete-students fear taking action to enact change in a system they deem far greater than themselves. First, they think, this is my family's hope. I'm headed to the NFL or NBA, and I can't do anything to endanger my scholarship.

Secondly, they don't want to be labeled as a troublemaker. Then there are those who simply don't care. They think, I'm only here for a short time. Whatever I do won't benefit me because I'll be gone by the time the rules change, so why even do anything? Why go through all of that? Ed says, "Most college athletes, including myself, always saw college as a stepping-stone to get to the NBA. So you think, whether I'm getting paid or not, if they're making money off my face, I'm going to make enough money at the next level anyway so I'll make it all back. I had that kind of mentality."[56]

Then you have athletes who think, *I'm not putting my life on the line so you feel good about your stance as a social activist. No, my family needs to eat. I'm not an activist, I just want to play ball and go home. I don't care about slavery or this compensation problem.* A lot of players don't care, and they have a right not to care because they're living for themselves. They truly believe that it's OK to be selfish.

---

[56]   Personal interview with Ed O'Bannon.

And that's the mantra for capitalists everywhere in America. When you're a capitalist country, it's about "get yours." Get yours! It's all about a mass of selfish and selfless people.

You have your selfless people who want to help, but don't want to risk it all. Then you've got selfish people who don't give a hoot about helping, don't care about anybody who's doing anything righteous, and are willing to do anything to protect what they have. Two dynamics that will always clash, simply because one person always wants it all and one person doesn't want anything. But both sides don't want to fight, for the greater good.

O'Bannon gives another reason that athletes will stay under the psychological control of the "massa." Ed says there are those who will risk putting their neck out there, who don't care about their own well-being. Say you're not afraid to step out and become a reform activist for the next generation of athletes. There is a downside to your actions. The resulting abuse directed at you often extends to the people around you. You as an individual can take the abuse and backlash. But it's the people close to you who didn't ask to be in this position. Your family. Your close friends and people who care about your well-being. How are they going to take verbal abuse and harassment from the hater out there? Those are things that you have to consider if you're going to speak out or stand up against injustice.

Penalties and Consequences of NCAA Rules

What do the following names have in common: Cam Newton, Johnny Manziel, Todd Gurley, Reggie Bush?

Cam Newton

In October 2011, the NCAA concluded a thirteen-month investigation into recruiting violations involving Newton at Auburn and found Auburn committed no major violations.

The NCAA agreed with Auburn's self-report from Nov. 30, 2010, that Cecil Newton Sr., Cam's father, and scouting service owner, Kenny Rogers, shopped Cam Newton's services to Mississippi State out of junior college, but that there was no evidence the player or Auburn knew about it.

Cecil Newton Sr. reportedly shopped his son's services to schools for up to one hundred and eighty thousand dollars. Auburn declared Newton ineligible four days before the Southeastern Conference (SEC) championship game, and the NCAA reinstated him the following day, saying there was not "sufficient evidence" that Cam Newton or Auburn knew of the attempts to cash in on his talent.[57]

Johnny Manziel

In August 2013, Manziel was suspended for the first half of the Texas A&M Aggies' season-opener against Rice due to evidence that he had received payment for signing autographs.

According to an NCAA representative, the NCAA and A&M agreed on a one-half game suspension because Manziel had violated NCAA bylaw 12.5.2.1, which says: student-athletes cannot permit their names or likenesses to be used for commercial purposes, including to advertise, recommend or promote sales of commercial products, or accept payment for the use of their names or likenesses.[58]

Todd Gurley

In 2014, the NCAA suspended Georgia running back Todd Gurley for four games. The school found that he had accepted "more

---

[57] http://www.espn.com/college-football/story/_/id/7093495/ncaa-finds-no-major-violations-auburn-regarding-cam-newton [AP, October 13, 2011]

[58] http://www.espn.com/college-football/story/_/id/9609389/johnny-manziel-texas-aggies-suspended-1st-half-season-opener-rice-owls

than $3,000 in cash from multiple individuals for autographed memorabilia and other items over two years." [59]

Reggie Bush

In 2010, the NCAA barred the Southern California Trojans' football program from bowl games in the 2010 and 2011 seasons. USC also had to vacate all victories in which Heisman Trophy winner Reggie Bush had participated, beginning in December 2004—including the Orange Bowl victory that produced the Trojans' Bowl Championship Series title in January 2005—and was docked ten scholarships in each of the next three seasons. [60]

Bush also had to give back his Heisman Trophy after it was found that he had accepted illegal gifts worth three hundred thousand dollars from marketing agents.

The ruling prompted many observers to rail against the perceived hypocrisy of the NCAA, which does not pay its players, but profits from their on-field achievements.

These high-profile players all allegedly violated NCAA rules through trying to make money off their own name and likeness, or by trying to get financial help from outside sources. As more and more rulings targeting certain players came down, athlete violations eventually started affecting universities. Universities started engaging in more academic fraud to cover up the players, to keep players on the rosters…so they could continue their eligibility…so they could still bring in the money. There is an illustrious history of cheating and penalties, player penalties and university consequences, throughout the entire existence of the NCAA. Usually the consequence to the

---

[59] https://www.sbnation.com/college-football/2014/10/29/7088883/todd-gurley-suspended-florida-kentucky-auburn

[60] http://www.nytimes.com/2010/06/11/sports/ncaafootball/11usc.html?mcubz=1

university is just a slap on the wrist, but when it comes to dealing with player violations, it affects their credibility, their reputation, their likability, and their draft status. Each one of these considerations plays a part in the athlete's demise when they get penalized for selling their own jersey, selling their own autograph, taking a suit for free, taking a sandwich for free, taking a ride for free. You can be penalized for doing anything similar to that, and your whole future can be put in jeopardy due to bullshit NCAA rules.

Nonprofit Sports

We already know the profit sports are football and basketball, but how is the university *system* different with nonprofit sports like wrestling, baseball, rowing, or rugby? If you get a scholarship in a nonprofit sport, you'll definitely have more leniency as an athlete-student than a profit-sport athlete-student because the demands of your sport don't have the same pressures of making a profit for the university. And since there are no pressures for making money for the university, you can focus on getting an education. But when you're dealing with high revenue-generating sports, it's a totally different ball game. There's enormous pressure on the coaches, the administration, the boosters, and often the alumni to make sure that year in and year out, they're always in the black when it comes to their investment. When you're a high-power football team like Alabama you have to make sure you have nothing but five-star athletes continually coming into the university because of the private money that's being spent in the state of Alabama. Those who are spending inordinate amounts of money do so because the return on investment is very high. Buying into university profit-sport programs is not being publicized as an investing option, so this is where we go back to the mob ties, where we have guys gambling inside an institution. It is a ripe situation where boosters and alumni all take their money to gamble and say, "Hey, if I spend a million dollars to help you build this facility, what percentage are you giving me back?" And the university says, "We're going to give you season tickets, we're going to make sure you're backstage, we're going to make sure you get memorabilia from all the national championships we have, and we'll give you a five percent kicker on all concessions or ticket sales at the game."

NCAA Tournament and College Football Series (CFS) Bowl Games

The NCAA Tournament and CFS are basically big-time showcases for the draft. Think back to stories of the slave trade, where they brought slaves up on a platform and auctioned them off. Or, all the slaves were in one boat and the masters and buyers were looking at each slave to pick which slave they wanted to buy. The slave owners didn't get to see the slaves doing their work; they didn't get to preview what the slaves could actually do.

On the contrary, the NCAA Tournament and CFS are showcases to preview talent. During these showcases, athletes can show the world what they can do and what coaches and team owners should look forward to in the next level, which is the professional level. The NCAA Tournament and CFS are big parties that cost enormous amounts of dollars; they're going to bring in big sponsors, various TV broadcast stations, drink companies, shoe companies, and car companies. According to financial writer Tim Parker in his Investopedia article,[61] on March Madness: "Last year the National Collegiate Athletic Association (NCAA) raked in a record $1 billion in revenue from media rights fees, ticket sales, corporate sponsorships and a proliferation of television ads anchored around the three-week long tournament." Andrew Soergel,[62] senior economy reporter for USNews.

---

[61] https://www.investopedia.com/articles/investing/031516/how-much-does-ncaa-make-march-madness.asp [Tim Parker, "How Much Does the NCAA Make Off March Madness," March 13, 2017]

[62] "The Money Behind the Bowl Games" [Dec. 23, 2014]

com, wrote: "Each Power 5 conference—the SEC, ACC, Big Ten, Big 12 and Pac-12—will rake in a base amount of $50 million this postseason, according to the College Football Playoff organization and the Alabama Media Group."

All these companies are going to pay the showcases an obscene amount of dollars to promote their big shows. The only thing is, the big shows are not paying any of the players. The showcases are strictly for the benefit of those running the show.

What's being told to the *talent* is, *We're showcasing you so the professionals [slave owners] can see you play and decide if they want to choose you or not. But there's no money involved in this particular review.* The people involved in this slave trade are getting paid handsomely while selling another lottery ticket dream: *Look, you guys are one step closer to your dream, keep at it. We're going to keep collecting our checks and you guys are going to keep thinking that your time is coming.* Do you see what's wrong with that picture? People are getting paid millions and millions of dollars and these hopeful kids, who are actually putting on the show, aren't getting paid. It's like grabbing for the proverbial carrot and never getting to it. The powers-that-be are thinking, *Okay, show's over; next rabbit.*

Boosters

Most university boosters' mission statements claim they are committed to providing educational and athletic opportunities for university athletes. They flaunt the fact that they support hundreds of outstanding athlete-students by giving them a chance to compete in college athletics while earning a world-class education from the university. See what the boosters are selling? A world-class education!

What's really being sold to boosters is: Come on and bring your mega money here, we're guaranteeing that these kids are getting educated. But we're not going to show you *how* they're getting educated. We're just going to tell you that ninety-two to ninety-four percent pass enough classes to graduate. And the athletes who graduate don't tell you *how* they passed enough classes to make it to graduation.

UNC's much-loved men's basketball coach, the late Dean Smith, coached UNC from 1961 to 1997. He proudly sold a ninety-six percent graduation rate to recruits, saying that their athletes always graduated, yet he failed to tell recruits *how* the athletic department managed to keep such a high rate. I'm telling you now that the reason the ninety-six percent graduation rate was able to stay so high is that, for almost thirty years, they had in place a grade system to make sure the guys graduated. Boosters are paying for that high percentage rate because that's what they're being sold, but it's not the real sales point. What's being sold is access to floor seats to the games, functions, and mixers so they can be around the players. They're sold a deal where they'll be able to meet the players and make them their favorite players. This is the way their investment pays off. As a booster, if a player knows you and you know him, you covertly give him a little envelope: it's like, *Here, take care of you and your family. Just remember my name when you get big.* You know what? He will remember who you are because you're the guy who gave him that money.

As Samuel Williamson, UNC provost and vice chancellor for academic affairs from 1984 to 1988, told Kenneth Wainstein, a former top U.S. Justice Department official, "Every time we closed the barn door, the athletics department built a new barn."[63] The "new barns" went beyond gut classes.[64] He included the 1980s summer school professor—soon relieved of his duties—who allowed athletes and others to finish a correspondence course in five days, and the four flunking football players who tried to retroactively withdraw after a bowl game for "medical reasons." At least twice, Williamson said,

---

63 https://www.si.com/college-basketball/2015/03/13/north-carolina-tar-heels-paper-classes-ncaa

64 Easy-to-pass classes

"Honor Court cases in the summer were not pushed because somebody said, 'It's going to hurt the guy's chances for a pro contract.'"[65]

Former UNC chancellor Holden Thorp, whose promising tenure was a casualty of the 2013 scandal, mused in *The News & Observer* about the new Tar Heels' reality. "*We thought we were different from Auburn,*" said Thorp,[66] "*but now we know that we're not.*"

Essentially, the boosters are being sold event production packages, or sponsorship packages. Those sponsorship packages have nothing to do with athletes getting a free education.

Any time you're in an investment deal, it's about: what am I getting back and how fast am I going to get it back?

---

[65] https://www.si.com/college-basketball/2015/03/13/north-carolina-tar-heels-paper-classes-ncaa (Unknown, 2015)

[66] http://www.newsobserver.com/sports/college/acc/unc/article1024 3649.html [Barry Jacobs, Feb. 1, 2015]

PHOTO GALLERY

1986. This picture depicts the future. I was 2 years old. No one could take away my dream. At least that's what I thought...

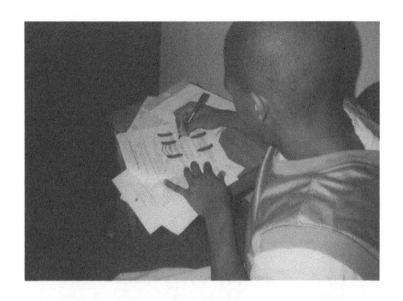

2002. Signing the NLI. No press conference. No lawyers. Just me and the librarian.

My first AAU state Championship with WNC Storm in 1998. I was MVP.

1995: My first time playing basketball for EMMA Elementary. Thank you Rick Smart!

My days at New Hampton Prep School.

The Late John Wooden and I during the 2002 McDonald's All American Game.

2001 early morning workouts. Jerell Lewis and I. This is where I became great. Thank you Ken Miller and Jamie Arsenault.

2005 NBA draft. This was the only goal I set out to accomplish: Shaking David Sterns hand and putting on that hat.

3RD QUARTER

The Problem with Plantation Education

Part II

7

Rashanda

Rashanda's story warrants its own attention, so within this chapter, she will share her own UNC experience, insights, and perspective.

Finding out about the whole paper class and fraud situation was honestly a shock for me. Unlike my brother's experience, mine was the complete opposite. I went to every class, I was always on time, I did all my work. I found out that later, after the allegations came out, and after the Wainstein Report(a 131-page investigative report by Kenneth Wainstein, a former top U.S. Justice Department official that made the strongest connection to date between the fake classes and athletes' eligibility), that none of the classes were actually legit, and that the person who was grading our classes never graded them. That part of finding out hit me really hard. I thought, how is it possible that I did the work, and you didn't grade it? The situation personally affected me because I could have enrolled for other courses. I thought, "You just wasted my time, and made me question every other class that I took." I questioned, were those teachers giving me As just because I was playing basketball? How much of this is real? That entire situation dunked me into the fraudulent class scenario.

I had taken all my classes within the AFRI-AFAM curriculum, headed by Julius Nyang'oro and Debbie Crowder. I took the classes offered, not knowing that they were the fraudulent classes. At the time, we [other athlete-students and I] thought that they were independent studies, but we did not know the classes were an easy, easy A. I was writing my papers and putting the time in, giving the papers to the instructor who I thought was a teacher, Debbie Crowder. To find out she actually was not a teacher made it even worse.

My major was in communications, but I could have minored in a few different areas; the transcripts for my other classes were all over the place. I had a few African-American studies, and a few psychology classes. All my classes were pretty scattered to the point where I was one or two credits away from minoring in a specific course of study, such as philosophy. I really didn't have one main focus except to major in communications.

I took two independent study courses, where we just wrote papers; Swahili is included within the courses. If anyone really went back and looked at the athlete-students in those two departments, AFRI-AFAM, Swahili is one language that most of us took, and we still don't know why we took it. We just knew it was part of the course, and, by the way, I did learn some Swahili, even though I've been hard-pressed to use it in everyday life. And even Swahili people don't speak Swahili.

In hindsight, why Swahili was even presented to us when Spanish or French should have been required first and second, is a mystery. My fellow athletes and I all wondered why the AFRI/ AFAM courses were offered when we were not benefiting from them in any way, shape, or form. Half of the United States is a Spanish-speaking nation, so the logical course of action would have been to take Spanish. But, again, Swahili was an easy solution—an easy A if you go back and look at any athlete-student's transcript. They will get either an A or a B in Swahili, and I never heard of anyone getting anything less than that.

It's no secret: college sports is a big moneymaker, and whenever you have money involved, the *system* itself is extremely hard to touch because the people you are trying to reach are pretty much untouchable. You have to go through so many avenues, and even with the NCAA, they're protected by way of their nonprofit structure. They imply in the Letter of Intent that they don't have anything to do with the school. They don't have anything to do with education. They say academics remains solely on the university. Then they reverse what they're saying, and they say, *Well, in order for you to play, you have to be eligible.* So that means they *do* have something to do with the education. It's very confusing from that standpoint, because when you play a profit-sport for the university, everyone [athletic departments, coaches, boosters] has to make sure that their players can play. And they all do whatever it takes. What goes unnoticed, for the most part, is that many universities have ADs (athletic directors), which is actually not an AD, but a student assistant. These student assistants are grad students, and they're teaching courses. The thing is, most grad students are still twenty-six to twenty-seven years old, and fans of whatever sport the athlete-students they're teaching play. So it's easy for them to overlook what's right and what's wrong and say, *Man, I'm a big fan of yours. You need help? I'll help you.*

Again, that's an oversight, but it is a big deal, because when I was in school, I had a whole bunch of student-teachers who were very easily impressed by me being an athlete, and wanted to help in any way possible. And the second part of that is just how big that movement is; it would be hard to touch because so many people are afraid to come forward. They're afraid of what they'll lose, they're afraid that what happened to my brother and I—being ostracized, kicked out and isolated from everything and everyone—will happen to them. But if the AD/student-teacher aspect was removed, it would be one of the biggest beasts that you'd take down for sure. Student-teachers are a big part of the mind-theft of the athlete-student's educational experience.

Just as the NFL's concussion settlement came about because of physical injury to the brain, universities are doing the same thing, only they're damaging athletes' brains through lack of education. There's no test, no postmortem, and no donating an athlete-student's brain to science due to a poor-quality education. There are facts, there are transcripts that prove athlete-students, especially black athlete-students, are receiving an inferior education; it's just a lot more difficult to prove. While you can see a physical injury, you can't see emotional injury.

In 2015, Devon Ramsay, former UNC football player, and I filed suit against the NCAA and the university for alleging that UNC purposefully pushed athlete-students "toward programs and courses that lacked rigor [and inflated grades] so as to free up as much time as possible for athletic commitments,"[67] effectively providing student-athletes with a less valuable education than that of the typical UNC student. A *Sports Illustrated* article reported: "Hausfeld [attorney for the case] demands the creation of an independent commission that would audit Division I programs to ensure that athletes are not victimized by academic fraud and that minority athletes are not receiving inferior education."[68]

We already know, based on the book *Cheated*, by Mary Willingham and Jay Smith, that many independent investigations have already been conducted, including the one by former North Carolina Governor Jim Martin, which resulted in more bogus con-

---

[67] https://www.huffingtonpost.com/2015/03/03/ncaa-north-carolina-academic-fraud_n_6792374.html [Maxwell Strachan, March 3, 2015]

[68] https://www.si.com/college-basketball/2015/01/06/rashanda-mccants-unc-paper-classes-lawsuit [Author Unknown, Jan. 6, 2015]

clusions, incomplete information, and cover-ups. We're all wondering what will make the new independent commission findings any different, and if the same people in the same positions will make it a point to hide the necessary records. How do you fix a problem whenever there's always going to be a cover-up, or someone is hired who has ulterior motives? If you're going to fix something, you have to take everyone who could potentially hide something and shuffle everything out the door, out of positions of power. Unfortunately, it's hard to say that above-board, honest, transparent answers will ever come because there are so many Carolina alums; secretly, privately, outwardly, there's so many people attached to the *system*.

UNC loyalty is the one thing with which you have to compete. I've seen many investigations and none of them have come out clear-cut. And even if different people are in positions of power, those positions are still going to release only certain information. They're going to hide certain information and I'm hoping that this independent commission, if enacted, will be different, and will be able to uncover new things or different things than have been uncovered in the past. One thing we all know for sure: money is power. Whoever holds the purse strings holds the power. Whenever you're in a financial position, you can make things go away. And that seems to happen very often at UNC.

Michael Hausfeld is seeking monetary damages for all former and current NCAA athletes who didn't receive the meaningful education they were promised by the NCAA conferences and member institutions. It will be an interesting day if that happens. It will be a day of victory for sure. The sole argument for most athletes, especially to my brother's point, is, you promised to educate us, and therefore you said you would not pay us because we are getting a free education. But whenever it is proved that you are not providing an education, it is extremely difficult to prove your case that you should not then pay us.

The bottom-line fact is: the NCAA has been in business for a long time, has a lot of power, and its money can probably last longer than anyone could imagine. So, who really knows if a victory will actually happen? Justice would be served if it did, but man, I would love to see the day that that monster is taken down and put back in its place.

There's the story of University of Central Florida (UCF) kicker Donald De La Haye, who had a YouTube channel that had nothing to do with the NCAA or the university, although it did have some athletics-related videos on a monetized account. De La Haye had a full scholarship as a football player, and the NCAA told him that he was ineligible because he was making money off a YouTube page. How do you penalize a person and his future for something that isn't benefiting you? It has nothing to do with the school. It has nothing to do with the NCAA. But you're going to tell this guy, *We own you. You're going to do what we say and you're not going to make a living until you're done. Until you've done your time.* Fortunately, De La Haye didn't submit to the plantation owners, but as a result, he was declared ineligible to play.

Conversely, the student body president of a university makes five thousand dollars a year for being the student body president. How come that doesn't make him a professional? That is insane to me. If I could have been a student body president making five thousand dollars a year, are you kidding me, in college while I was struggling to get by? It would be doubly crazy if that person was an athlete-student. Then, that person would be in direct violation of NCAA regulations while being penalized for being academically sound in every aspect of the university. The system is set up to penalize athlete-student academic achievement. That's what it feels like, anyway. Choose one or the other. Either you're going to be OK at academics, or you're going to be excellent in your sport.

I have to add here that there are athlete-students in legitimate majors, like a business major, who go to every single one of their classes and get their grades and do it the way it's designed, but you have to put into perspective exactly *how* they're able to accomplish that feat. On the women's basketball team, we had walk-ons, players who didn't play a lot, and then you had the stars. *Voilà*—behold the difference. That's where it gets tricky, because when you look at the top five players, who are depended on every game for consistently high performance: their academic standards are much lower. They wouldn't be able to go on to be a doctor or a lawyer because they need to focus so much time and effort on their talent while in school. But then you have those six players, or seventh player, or eighth player, who the coaches don't really care if they get in the game or not. Those athlete-students would rather go to classes, get their education, and the coach doesn't care if they have an exam that day because their role within the structure of the team isn't considered as essential to overall team success. I want to make it clear, though: the nonstarters were just as important to the success of the team as a whole, but there was less pressure on them than the starters.

But with that star player, it's like, *Man, we got to figure out a way to have you retake that test.* Or *we have to figure out a way to get you there and get you to the game.* There's more pressure on that star player than on the player who isn't as recognized. And that's a very, very, big point because it matters. The less recognized players can say, *Oh, I went to all my classes.* To that I would respond, *You went to class, sure, and you did all your work, sure, but were you the star player? Did the coaching staff care if you went to class? Yes, or no?*

See the difference?

I have to say that my coach, Sylvia Hatchell, and my assistant coach, Andrew Calder, for sure were very involved in all our academic standings and making sure we went to class. I can't say anything negative about them holding us accountable for going to class. And I can say that that's why I was so upset to find out that so much academic fraud happened at the university, because of how adamant my coaches were about us going to class and making sure we were doing everything right. And that's where that whole "*Cheated*" aspect comes into play. It's like, man, who knew? We were doing what we thought was right—going to classes, studying, only to find out in the end that they were bogus, fluff classes.

If any reform is to take place, you would have to start at the middle school level because that is where it all starts, and really even before that because the AAU is starting earlier and earlier. The middle school is where kids are being targeted as being athletic or being pretty good players. But then high school, I think, is the primary focus, because that's when you are challenged. High schools have AP courses, and if you're not in an AP class, why aren't you there? It's like, what part of that don't you get? And then there's also the fact that they don't pay teachers enough to really care that much at the high school level. That means you have a lot of kids who get lost in the shuffle because there's one teacher for thirty students. Then when you go to college, there's one teacher for fifty students. If I couldn't learn at the thirty-student standard, how am I going to learn in the fifty- or sixty-student standard?

The question then becomes, *How did you even get to this university? You can't read. How did you get here if you can't read? Now that you're here and you still can't read, how are you still eligible?* Reform would come in the form of saying, *how do we get to the athletes sooner; what would we have to do in high school to hold the high school teachers accountable for this athlete-student?* And, if there is money involved, or if the kid can't afford something, what stipend are you going to provide for motivation? Because a lot of times it's lack of motivation to care. The athlete-students may think, *I'm going to be out of the league in a year, so I don't really care.*

I started playing basketball when I was in the third grade. In fact, I played a sport from the third grade all the way up until I was twenty-six. By the time I was in the eighth grade, I was getting recruited by colleges. At the time, I didn't even know what that meant. But now it's even worse—the AAU is starting earlier and earlier. And again, it's one of those things where you just have to filter the nonperforming students out sooner, and know exactly where that student is, and hold him or her accountable, hold their parents accountable, and hold the school accountable. That's the hard part. As we've seen, the educational conveyor belt does get out of control.

Parents become as much a part of the system as anyone else.

I think they should be compliant, but at the same time, often working parents simply don't know what's happening. They get their kids' report cards and they see they're doing well, at least most of the time. When schools hold parent-teacher conferences, parents often aren't able to make it, so they don't know how well their kids are really doing, nor do they have time to actually go in and investigate.

For athlete-students, the challenge lies primarily in high school because you're old enough to know better, you're old enough to know what you're supposed to be doing, and you know right and wrong. If you just don't understand something, that's a whole other story. When I used to mentor kids when I was in the WNBA, especially athletes, there's this thing where you play stupid in the classroom. It's seen as a cool thing to play like you don't know what you're talking about when you know very well everything the teacher is saying. The playing dumb part is a very strong impulse, especially socially when it comes to peer pressure. You might say, "I'm going to go do my homework or read a book." Your friend or someone else picks on you. "What? Why would you go do that? Have somebody do it for you."

I was recently asked, "Knowing what you know now, would you do anything different?" Being older now, you really reflect on a lot of things that you just didn't know when you were a kid, and I think that's the scary part. What happened to my brother and myself, and many others, is that we were kids, and it was always the responsibility of the grown-up to protect us and guide us in the right direction. And to know that the grown-ups had ulterior motives, or that they wanted to use you as a way to get somewhere, that part is very frustrating. If I were to go back in time and do it all over again, I would pay much more attention and focus on what I wanted to do. When I was sixteen, seventeen, eighteen, I had no clue what I wanted to do professionally. And honestly, today, I still feel scattered. I still kind of don't know what I want. I'm all over the place. I want to do everything. They put pressure on you by the time you're a junior in college that you need to figure out what your major is, and if you do actually figure out your major in your junior year, you have one year to fit all of it in. But when you're an athlete, you not only have one year to fit it all in, you also have the pressure of whether you're going to make it to the league or not.

You struggle with secondary thoughts: *Okay, is playing in the pros something I'm going to do long-term?* For me, it turned out to be a waste of time to go to a pro league. I don't want to discredit the WNBA or anything, but when I look back at everything that I've done, I make more money now than I did in the WNBA by working my way up from sales to auto business finance, and now business manager. And if I had focused more while I was in college on being a business person or having my MBA, I could be a president, vice president, or CEO of a company that I interned at, or something similar. All I know is that I could be making three times the money that I'm making now. That's the only thing that I would go back in and try to refocus on; I would try to do something that would actually benefit me once I left school.

4TH QUARTER

Solutions for Plantation Education

8

I've talked a lot about the problems within the *system* surrounding college athletics, but I would be doing a disservice by not proposing some solutions. Most solutions cannot be implemented overnight; they take time and include enormous effort by athlete-students, both current and alumni, as well as athlete-student advocates, activists, attorneys, and those who truly want to see a comprehensive overhaul of the university/NCAA system. Without change, athlete-students will continue to be exploited and harvested for their talent with nothing to show for it except a beat-up body, inferior education, no marketable skills, and a nominal existence.

Based on my experience, knowledge, and research, as well as input from other prominent figures in the sports/academic industry, there are numerous viable options that could enable athlete-students to better navigate their university experience without being robbed of an education and a future.

Abolish the NLI

I've talked a lot about the problems with the NLI in Chapter Six but, again, stating the problem does no good unless there is a solution. According to a sports.vice.com article:[69]

"If you're an elite talent, you don't need to sign a letter of intent to receive an athletic scholarship. A basic financial aid agreement with the school of your choice will do.

"More to the point, you'll be putting your signature on what Andy Staples of *Sports Illustrated* rightly calls 'the worst contract in America'—a one-sided agreement that snuffs out your bargaining leverage, doesn't fully guarantee you a scholarship, and could put you and your family in a major bind if you happen to change your minds between now and the start of the college preseason."

The article goes on: "'The original intent of the letter is valid,' says Warren Zola, a sports law expert and Boston College professor. 'A school offers a spot for a player, it comes with a scholarship, you want some level of commitment from both sides, and this piece of paper offers that. The problem is that they are preposterously one-sided.'"

Later in the article, Hruby states, "Historically, the college sports establishment's attitude toward expanding rights and benefits for athletes has been simple: Hell fucking no. The NCAA fights tooth and nail for amateurism, an arguably illegal system of inarguable economic control; player-friendly reforms such as cost-of-living stipends and the ability to even offer four-year scholarships have come only as a result of legal defeats and public shamings."

Coaches aren't required to sign NLIs, or any other contract of intent, so why should athlete-students?

---

69   https://sports.vice.com/en_us/article/pgn38z/why-top-ncaa-recruits-shouldnt-sign-national-letters-of-intent (Patrick Hruby, "Why Top NCAA Recruits Shouldn't Sign National Letters of Intent," Sports.vice.com, Feb. 1, 2017)

Create a Unionized Athlete Council
to Protect Athletes' Rights

A unionized athlete council would basically involve creating a union that provides consultation to all young athletes headed into college. Whenever there's talk of unionizing, everybody freaks out and an uproar ensues. Those on the front line who propose and support unionizing would need to be steadfast in holding their ground, as they would be mentally and emotionally character-assassinated by the powers-that-be for even suggesting that standing up for more representation for the athlete-student is needed. There has to be some type of united front where there's a voice speaking for the athlete.

Antitrust economist Andy Schwarz states, "The NCAA does not see itself as a protector of athletes' rights to an education but rather as a sort of Owners Union protecting the sports product sold by schools and serving to cartelize wages. End the cartel and recharter the NCAA as a true protector of athletes' rights (or empower another organization like a trade association to do so) and then competition will result in athletes getting strong protections, such as contracts, that guarantee them real access to educational services, not just paper classes."[70]

As historian Taylor Branch said, start with the athletes' rights and the rest just flows naturally. The economic rights of college athletes have been disregarded. Give them back and then let the system push towards justice—one of the economic benefits will be that the education provided will rise to the same value given to other customers of the university.

Speaking of athletes' rights, Ed O'Bannon expresses, "I believe basketball and football should have the same draft rules as hockey and baseball, which are predominantly white sports. University athletes in basketball and football should have representation and

---

[70] Personal interview with Andy Schwarz.

be able to get drafted right out of high school. And the rules should also state that if the student-athlete doesn't like their draft status they can go back to school on a scholarship."[71]

Treat Athletes like Regular Students

Sonny Vaccaro says, "Treat an athlete just like a regular student coming to your school. Let him register, let him pick his classes, give him support that he should have through the academics provided by the university. These are things that are a given for education. As it stands, athlete-students can't do that because they have to be at practice at 5 in the morning or 3 in the afternoon. They have to leave on trips on Tuesday, or if they're in the NCAA tournament, the football playoffs, or whatever sport, they're constantly traveling for months at a time so all they get are papers that someone gives them and they fill out in the back room with mentors or proctors. They should be treated as what the NCAA and universities want to call them, a regular student. Let them come in and use the name Joe Blow, and then just go register; we'll tear it off like it's a lottery ticket and that will be his name, and that's the class he's going to take."[72]

Sports Education Programs

Sports education for athletes is the one thing missing when it comes to information, management, development, and understanding. There is a business for doctors, there's a business for lawyers, hell, there's even a business for business. There's business school, there's law school, and there's med school. There should be a sports school to serve as a whole new brand of education for athletes to allow us a new pathway to postgraduate courses. You need a place where you can learn more about sports, whether you want to be an agent, a manager, a sports trainer, a scout, or a coach. Sports education

---

[71]   Personal Interview with Ed O'Bannon.
[72]   Personal Interview with Sonny Vaccaro.

would operate from a single department. If this were instituted, I believe there would be a decrease in so many one-and-done athletes, and a decrease in the number of professional athletes going broke after two or three years. A sports business program would cover money management, financial breakdowns, media training, and all crucial areas of sports education that don't exist right now—at least not under one roof and one department. That is why no athlete is really taking advantage of or monetizing a culture that spends two trillion dollars a year in the market. That's a ton of spending power.

A sports-specific education program would be completely performance-based, which would put more of an onus on coaches to teach these athletes sports education. Currently, the coach is getting paid millions of dollars to *not* do anything that's required by the university. Under my reformed system, the university would put the responsibility on the coach to make sure athletes participate in the required performance-based courses, which would allow the coach to get to know his players more; there would be development going on within the process.

As the players develop from semester to semester, coaches would observe a unique difference in each player in the form of results. Those results could then be checked, and then re-surfaced to promote and push towards the professional level of NBA and MLB, showing results of progression by an athlete from the moment he arrives at the university to the moment he leaves.

The athlete's progression creates more data that's more efficient in showing who is ready to play in the pros and those who have the performance peak to move forward outside of basketball, or any sport. If a player does not experience as much performance-based success as others, the coaches and professors would then steer his attention toward coaching, media training, or maybe a field in management or finance. Coaches and the university would have the results to sit down with this kid and say, *Look, your weak points are here, your strong points are here; it seems like you're best suited to go in this [or that] direction.* Consulting with the student on where to go in life outside of sports and how to maneuver to get there would be part of the overall strategy. Grooming athlete-students to excel on the sports business side also creates more job opportunities in the sports field, which would force us to create more football leagues, more baseball leagues, and more basketball leagues. With those new leagues would be more jobs, and with more jobs there would be more athletes in coaching, training, and development positions, rather than former athletes just sitting around without having any real education. Former athletes don't always know where to go; we're often just sitting around waiting for each other to fail.

There's a lack of black men in professional sports in head coaching spots and ownership positions, so having a sports education program would really open doors for players to develop into leadership roles. It would also position coaches to be involved in the development of athlete-students beyond the sports arena; coaches would take it as a challenge to be more receptive in developing their players. Other coaches would take it as a hit because they haven't a clue about how to govern a program like that or how to communicate with athletes beyond telling them what to do on the field or court. Now, the coach says whatever he wants to the players and reaps the benefits of the success of the team. A sports education program would force the coach to show that what he's teaching and doing has results attached. Even now, with performance-based results, we see players getting better under a particular coach because that coach now has a responsibility to teach these kids what they need to be taught to get to the next level.

With a sports education program in place, we'd be able to prove the true amateurs are the coaches and, as a result, not allow them to get paid a bunch of money just for who they are. You would actually have to show us real results. If a guy like Roy Williams is making it to the finals, but none of his players is reaching performance-based peaks, it will be evident that there is something going on with the system. We would be able to tell the carryover from players in a winning tournament and then making it in the NBA; the results are not there. Something is not right.

The bottom line is that athlete-students are not being properly developed for operating a professional business. Athletes aren't valued at the same level as a lawyer, doctor, or businessman, yet professional athletes make twice as much money as most of those professions put together. However, performing on the field or court isn't regarded as a skill that needs a formal education. Being viewed as professionals would increase the value of the athlete's ten-cent brain because athletes would have a sports-specific education outside of a systematic K-12education. After high school, if an athlete doesn't meet the requirements of a top university, he should be able to attend a school of sports to qualify for that university, or there should be eligibility requirements in high school for sports education that could help them get into major universities without cheating or receiving false grades. Why would an athlete be ushered into AFAM or other designed-for-eligibility paper classes to boost his GPA when sports education classes can better inform him about sports and the career field in which he plans to embark? The answer lies in the true essence of what the purpose of a university is for an athlete.

The definitive solution for a sports education program is in my vision for The Legacy Center, a mega sports complex that would include:

- Multipurpose arena and auditorium for sporting events, concerts, exhibitions, trade shows, festivals, conventions (twenty-four luxury box suites)
- VIP private practice facility
- Fitness performance center with fitness machines, weight training, and boxing area as well as a rock-climbing wall

- Exhibit halls/banquet rooms for themed events, banquets, nonprofit benefit events, and parties
- Sports education learning center with fifteen-plus classrooms for educational and arts-related programs, library/literacy room, and sports academy
- Virtual business center space, leased office space, and meeting/conference rooms
- Vendor space for apparel, merchandise, juice bar, massage room, GNC/vitamin store
- Structured and surface parking
- Academy dormitories
- Dance and wellness studio
- Legacy Center Museum and Gift Shop featuring memorabilia from legendary North Carolina natives who have made iconic strides in film/TV, sports, arts, media, and the social/political arena.
- Legacy Walk: bricks would be purchased by community and celebrity donors to represent civic responsibility and to perpetuate and celebrate the success of our youth.

Future expansion plans would include:

- Family Fun Center (with arcade, trampoline area, party rooms, bowling, sports-themed activities, and sports bar and grill). Think Dave & Busters.
- Batting cages and equipment rental facility
- Two multipurpose fields and stadium
- Clubhouse for outdoor sports and events
- Playground/fitness park with after-school child development/daycare space
- Trail around entire property for biking, walking, and cross-country

A facility of this caliber would not only fuel athletic talent and provide ongoing sports education to athletes and the public, it also would provide jobs in the athletic space; engage families in the athletic experience; encourage entrepreneurialism through the apparel, merchandise, and concession stands; provide revenue from across the country and globe; and deliver cutting-edge, top-shelf performance training for athletes of all ages, especially preventative care training for youth to reduce injuries and to speed recovery when injuries do happen.

Performance-based Compensation Requirements

Performance-based compensation refers to the athlete's accountability. The athlete now has accountability during his performance-based requirements to perform, show up, and make sure that he doesn't have the pressures of being an academic-required athlete; he now has a performance-based requirement that he can completely focus on without the rigors of waking up in the morning, thinking about English, math, or psychology. The athlete's focus is strictly on weights, speed, and strength, and his only thoughts are, *I have to be able to shoot this three.* Now the focus and the accountability are on the athlete. You don't act on the performance-based requirements, then you don't get that extra funding that comes wrapped in that scholarship, which acts as your compensation because that's the only way you can really bring in additional funds without being guilty or crossing the lines of the NCAA. The athlete can then have funds set up through the university that pays him for his likeness and name being used by the university, broadcasting companies, magazine companies, and video game companies, with a percentage of that revenue going to the athlete's account. The athlete would get not only a percentage from using his likeness, but a percentage of ticket sales, as well as a percentage of the concession. The athlete's account is held in escrow until he uses up all his desired eligibility. Whether he completes four years of school, or his performance-based requirements have been reached, he can then go on to the next level. If that athlete decides to forfeit his eligibility, his trust fund can be opened and used after a particular limit of time.

That means an athlete-student coming into a university would not have to take the basic classes of English, math, and language because they have taken those subjects the last twelve years of their life in K-12. That's where they got their basic information. The rudimentary information that you're served when you get to college is really just a recap of what you learned over the last twelve years. If we eliminate the basics and jump right into sports performance, we give the athlete an option after he uses his eligibility for the sports side. If you use up all your eligibility, you can come back and use that eligibility for academic purposes. Current and retired coaches and sports experts would be the class instructors. I propose to make classes more digital and visual, where experts conduct webinars and seminars that teach athlete-students (in a virtual environment), so there's not just one person at each school teaching a bunch of students who are only thinking about getting out of class and making it to practice on time. The course work could be accessible online, but still contain structures where instructors are telling students exactly what to do as far as skill sets and development. Then we'd bring in instructors and/or teaching assistants to actually facilitate those courses.

As far as ongoing self-education for core subjects like reading, math, and other basic skills, anyone can sign up for free online tutoring sites, from GCFlearnfree.org or low-cost learning sites like Lynda.com.

Professor Billy Hawkins asserts, "Reduce the commercial pressure that has been placed on the shoulders of the athletes in revenue-generating sports who are predominantly black males. Or, reduce the academic demands required of them during the semester of their competition. For example, instead of twelve hours of course work, give them the option of taking three to six hours, especially athletes who may have some academic challenges coming into the institution. They can take additional hours during the summer to keep on track with graduating in four to five years.[73]

Multiple Scholarship Opportunities for Athletes

As athlete-students, we would be able to receive one scholarship from the university where we would play our sport, but then we'd be able to receive additional scholarships from churches, tax-exempt organizations (or 501(c)(3)s), and other nonprofits that can provide us with supplementary funding. Currently, the system allows you to receive only one scholarship from the specific university where you play. Most people believe they can get only one scholarship, but there are multiple scholarships given by several entities.

The NCAA would probably accept this since the NLI is a voluntary contract. Knowing that you don't have to sign the NLI, you could receive multiple scholarships that would bring in multiple sources of financial funding. You could receive an academic scholarship from a church that gives you twenty-five thousand dollars to take care of your books, or from a private nonprofit that wants to support black athlete-students, or any of the other scholarship programs like Scholarship America.[74]

Insure Athletes with a Workers' Compensation Plan

Athlete-students, especially in high-impact sports like football, are "shown the door" by the university as soon as they sustain a major injury and can't play any longer. Scholarship gone. Education gone. Medical bills for that injury, which can last for

---

[73] Personal interview with Billy Hawkins.
[74] https://scholarshipamerica.org/

decades, become solely the responsibility of the athlete-student and his family. After all, the athlete-student was recruited because of his athletic ability, and when that ability is curtailed, the athlete is no longer of use to produce profits for the university and the NCAA. Jason Belzer, sports attorney and founder of GAME, Inc., a company specializing in the career management and marketing of coaches, asserts in a 2013 *Forbes* article:[75] "If we closely examine the relationship between scholarship athletes and their universities, from a legal prospective [sic], the argument could be made that they are really 'employee athletes.'" Belzer reiterates a well-known fact: "Universities retain the right to unilaterally terminate an athletic scholarship without liability."

In his 2015 article, "Can College Athlete Get Workers' Comp?—The Northwestern Case,"[76] attorney Matt Groganstates, "Workers' compensation for college athletes is especially necessary for those players who incur substantial injury that requires years of rehabilitation. Under most state law (Maryland's included), workers' compensation covers 100 percent of medical bills for employees who are injured on account of their jobs. However, unless a student-athlete is literally paralyzed while competing on behalf of his or her university, the NCAA permits schools to cut ties with former players once they are no longer students."

Matt continues later in the article that, in many cases, "Lingering medical issues continue far beyond the end of a student-athlete's enrollment. In such cases, the burden to pay for continuing medical treatment falls squarely on the former players themselves, oftentimes resulting in a lifetime of debt. Given the fact that the NCAA is a billion-dollar business that profits off the back of its players, you tell me if this seems fair?"

---

[75] https://www.forbes.com/sites/jasonbelzer/2013/09/09/leveling-the-playing-field-student-athletes-or-employee-athletes/#685b787852a1

[76] http://www.baltimorecomplawyer.com/blog/northwestern-case/

Crowdfunding Sources

Another possible solution for providing athlete-students with funding is crowdfunding. Websites like GoFundMe would work well in this arena, but an even better option would be a website specific to athlete-students. This type of funding source hasn't been tapped into yet. It would be preferable if a crowdfunding site could be set up specifically for athletes so that fans and companies know that a particular crowdfunding[77] site is only for athlete scholarships.

According to a 2017 sportsengine.com article on crowdfunding,[78] it seems that the NCAA still has their paws in the process. They put so many stipulations on it that it still creates a stranglehold for the athlete, although it does open a small door to funding sources.

Require Athletes Three Years of Compensated Experience

The first three years is basically creating the college football model for all athletes who are participating at high-revenue universities. If you're a profit-sport football or basketball player, you should receive guaranteed compensation for the first three years, which allows for an improved business model for the professionals bringing in more talent. If you're bringing in one-and-done young talent, and after three years you see the league is full of one-and-done players, the league is going to diminish quite a bit because the incoming players lack experience. Having three years of compensated experience creates greater opportunity for college athletes to promote and showcase their talents on the professional level, as well as allowing more money to be generated for the professional

---

[77] http://community.sportsengine.com/news_article/show/743030
[78] NCAA approves crowdfunding for student-athletes, when adhering to guidelines

leagues because they have more seasoned talent, and that brings in more dollars for the fan base.

Pro leagues are bringing in college guys with whom fans have become familiar during his three years of playing at the university. If you have a guy coming out of high school like Kobe Bryant, and you didn't see him play before he went pro, you just hear this guy is good. Then when you get to see him play, he doesn't have a fan base like you would think because he's fresh out of high school.

When you have a guy who's been in college three years, like Shane Battier, for instance, people are going to be more prone to watch Shane because: 1) he played at Duke, 2) he played at Duke for three years, and 3) he was a National Player of the Year candidate. You now have more people willing to pay money to go see Shane Battier play in the pros than they would to pay to see Kwame Brown, who was drafted by the Washington Wizards in 2001, straight out of high school. Shane has more fans, and more fans mean more conversion rate of profit. That's the mentality of the business deal: *We want more developed players to come into our workplace because it's going to bring us more fans. If we don't, we're going to suffer because the guys we do let into the league don't have enough name or story line for us to sell to make people come see these players*. That is what is currently happening to the NBA right now. There aren't enough fans who know the players coming into the NBA; therefore, they are stuck in an old model of basically cheering for guys they don't know because there are no new known guys to cheer for.

What happens in the first three years is that the athlete who is being used and compensated for his likeness is not only well-versed in what to do *with* his money, but he has *enough* money with which to do something. That's the point of being compensated for the first three years, but after that three years is up, the athlete-student actually has money in his pocket and something to show for all his effort. He's not stressed, he's not broke, and he has some money he can walk away with from going to college.

You went to college for a reason, you got paid while you were doing it, and now you have some money to move around with, invest with, or make a living. Not only have you made some money, but you should also be able to pursue other options outside of sports. The money would not be handed over to the athlete-student at his whim to just drain it dry so that he's starting over post-college with nothing. It's held safely in an escrow account, which is managed by an athlete-counsel. The counsel would be responsible for consulting with athletes about what they're going to be using their money for outside of the scholarship. When you want to take money out of your escrow account, you have to consult with your athlete-counsel about how you're going to use the money.

The escrow account system would allow you to take a portion of your money out whenever you want to go home and visit your sick mom, or just to see your family for the weekend, buy Christmas presents, or whatever it is you want to do. On the professional level, when you're dealing with a financial advisor, those are the exact same steps you're going to have to use when dealing with your own money.

As an athlete-student, your funds would have to be strategically placed in an escrow account to accumulate interest until that time when you want to forfeit and take your money out. Also, if the university or athlete-counsel within the university holds it, it's not going to be under the control of one individual, where bad things can sometimes happen. You've all heard stories about unscrupulous financial advisors who disappear in a hurry with their clients' money. A larger entity in charge of funds, with checks and balances, would eliminate misappropriation of funds, and provide a level of accountability for the athlete-student.

Professor Hawkins notes, "Compensate athletes at fair cost for their athletic labor; they are being paid with an athletic scholarship but it is not fair compensation. Some of this cost-cutting and increasing the compensation to athletes will come at a cost to coaches' salaries. For example, to give a monthly stipend of one thousand dollars for eighty to one hundred athletes on a football team will cost an athletic department around one million dollars. Well, if they don't want to cut into their surplus funds, they may have to look in other areas, and one of the areas is coaching salaries."[79]

Antitrust attorney Michael Hausfeld says this in response to proposing a compensation system be set up in order to create equitable yet safe-guarded financial funding: "To the extent that when they're minors, there are many ways of setting up trusts. With regard to the argument that they'll blow the money, think about this: there are no restrictions on how those older white males who are in charge of the organization blow their money. What has to happen is the control by the NCAA over the revenue needs to be broken so the market determines how the revenue gets shared and how the universities have to compensate their athletes. We also need to get the academic community to make adjustments and adopt reforms to give the students who happen to be athletes the same quality education and opportunities that they give non-athlete students. Compliance departments, athletic departments, and student advisors all need to be reined in. This is a major issue that has to be addressed at the national university level, and in the courts if necessary. This problem is far from being over and we will continue to pursue any legitimate and appropriate judicial means of correcting these injustices."[80]

---

[79] Personal interview with Billy Hawkins.
[80] Personal interview with Michael Hausfeld.

Setting Up Job Opportunities in Advance

Since the athlete-student's university life has been focused on performing on the field or court, he has not taken the time to think about what he will do afterward if he does not go to the pros. There's a real advantage in setting up job opportunities before he leaves the university. It would greatly benefit the athlete-student to have on the table vocational opportunities including college coaching, college fitness, self-employment, or other revenue-producing career paths. In addition, the student-athlete should be trained in interviewing and job search skills so he can pursue job opportunities in a variety of businesses.

Creation of More Semi-professional Leagues and Associations

Sports leagues in and of themselves are a subculture, so creating more semi-pro leagues, fitness centers, recreational centers, and sports-related associations can create player, coaching, and training opportunities. Anything in the realm of sports that can be created and started by players will provide the resources to create our own society.

In fact, a new league making its presence known is the HB (Historical Black College) League,[81] which started in 2018. Its founders are Andy Schwarz; Richard J. Volante, attorney at Buckley King LPA in their Sports, Entertainment, and Media Practice Group; and Bijan C. Bayne, an award-winning Washington-based freelance columnist, critic and author of *Sky Kings: Black Pioneers of Professional Basketball*. According to the HB website, its mission statement is a far cry from the stench of NCAA confinement:

> The League mission is to create a thriving, commercial basketball league focused on improv-

---

[81]   http://hbleague.com

ing the educational and career opportunities for African Americans. We also have the goal of changing the landscape of collegiate athletics by providing college athletes with the ability to receive educational opportunities without acquiescing to a collective agreement to provide payment for their athletic abilities.

LaVar Ball, the Kunta Kinte of a new era, is creating a league for high school athletes who want to forgo the college experience. Ball calls his new league The Junior Basketball Association. Ball has said the league will be fully funded by his Big Baller Brand, including paying salaries ranging from three thousand dollars to ten thousand dollars a month depending on a player's status. Players will naturally don Big Baller Brand (BBB) shoes and uniforms since BBB is promoting the league. Ball has also stated that the rules of his league will follow those of the NBA instead of standard college rules. Ball admits that there is much to do before the league premieres, but it will certainly provide a much-needed alternative for young athletes who don't want to attend college.

In addition, in a bold move, the two younger Ball brothers, LaMelo and LiAngelo, took their talent overseasinstead of bowing to the NCAA plantation. They each signed one-year deals to play with the Lithuanian club Vytautas Prienai and, by doing so, demonstrated their belief that they can make their money overseas, and come back and pay for their own education in the U.S. without succumbing to the NCAA cartel. As more semi-professional leagues pop up in the U.S., young athletes are able to stay closer to home and utilize their talent here while calling their own educational shots.

Sports Transition Programs for Former Athletes

Sports transition programs will basically teach former athletes who were left behind and left out in terms of financial, business, and educational literacy, and reengage them back into sports education programs. These transitional programs will effectively place them back into the system of getting specialized information on the career path they choose.

Pasha Cook is author of *Champs U: Guide to Championing Athletic Transition*. She coaches athletes on how to navigate the waters of transition from college and/or pro sports to the "real" world, and shows them how to effectively brand themselves in their post-career. Pasha tells athletes that a lot of sports transition is psychological. As a professional athlete, you're getting a huge salary. You're getting the perks. You're getting all these accolades because of your job title. You're a forward or center or whatever for this or that college or in the NBA. Now that you're a regular person and you're not getting the accolades and sports hero-worship from the public, you don't know who you are. Pasha teaches her athlete clients who they are as individuals and helps them discover the innate talent they possess, as well as what they learned during their athletic career that can translate into a successful post-sports life.

Federal, State, and Regionally-funded Compensation Programs for Athletes

The government and state in which each university is located should get involved in providing funds for additional scholarship programs that offer more opportunities for athletes. State, regional, and national funding programs are already in place and pay the universities, so we would ask for those funds to be split up for athletes instead of being paid to the coaches because the state already pays the coach.

Along the line of federal compensation, Ed O'Bannon shares his take on a different kind of federal involvement: "The NCAA thinks they're so incredibly powerful that they pretty much have supreme reign to do whatever the hell they want to do. A federal governmental entity needs to tell the NCAA, 'Okay, we're going to hand out government sanctions.'"[82]

Establish Athletes as Independent Contractors

When you're a third-party contractor, you're being contracted for your services, which for the athlete-student is being fully dedicated to playing a sport. If a third-party contractor is providing services directly to the university, it would intentionally get rid of or discourage any academic requirements. Athletes would basically be contracted to play sports at their university. We wouldn't have to go to class. We wouldn't have to live on campus. None of those things. We would literally just show up for practices and games—similar to semi-pro. College sports would turn into semi-professional.

The NCAA would be pushed out of the process completely and every university would then act independently outside of the NCAA. The NCAA would be involved for the NCAA tournament. If the athletes ever decide to unite and be part of an independent contractor system, the NCAA wouldn't be forced to make changes. It would be forced to either be a part of that system or lose money—lose money or lose the players. The NCAA can't afford to lose the players; all it would have to do is negotiate.

Mary Willingham states, "So if we dismantle the NCAA as a member institution organization, and the NCAA just exists as being in charge of the tournaments, they'll still make a lot of money, and I think they do a really good job in running the tournaments and getting all those TV contracts, but I just believe that athletes need a share, like profit sharing as independent contractors. Athletes also need to decide if education is important to them. To be clear about what institution you're academically eligible to study at so

---

[82]   Personal interview with Ed O'Bannon.

that you can get a real education. So in other words, if you're not ready for Carolina, but you want to go to Carolina, you'll have to do some community college to get ready, or something similar. Whatever regular students have access to."[83]

If the players decide to play and they are getting compensated nationally or funded locally or regionally, then there is no reason for universities to pay the NCAA. Each university in each division in each conference pays the NCAA fees to be a part of the NCAA so that it can participate in the NCAA tournament. The fees universities pay are small investments for participating in tournaments. If you win, you get a bigger piece, a bigger chunk of that fee you put in. It's like playing cards. Everybody has to pay to play. If you don't make it to the tournament, we're sorry, but you need to invest better in your athletes. Those who make it to the tournament, now you have a chance to hit the power ball. Now that you're part of the NCAA tournament, you're part of the power ball tournament. Whoever wins the national tournament is the power ball winner.

The NCAA needs to be left with no choice. Athletes, universities, and athlete-councils have to have all their ducks in a row when it comes to understanding what the NCAA needs. They need us. They need athletes onboard. They need to make sure there's no competition or competitors. Thus far, we have given them everything they've ever wanted. We give them competitors. We give them the ability to unionize.

Now athlete-students have unions set up, we have counsels set up, and we have funding set up—even if the athletes decide not to go to college. And if an athlete decides not to go to college, we will have facilities for him to get specialized education and training, and still make it to the pros without going to college.

---

[83] Personal interview with Mary Willingham.

The initial setup of an independent contractor system would have to be done covertly. It wouldn't have to be done in a physical sense. It would need to be an elaborate, carefully designed blueprint that would be a no-brainer for the NCAA to completely agree to and fall in line. I was quoted as saying that UNC[84] is going to pay me ten million dollars and the NCAA is going to pay me three hundred million dollars, but, as usual, it was taken out of context. What I'm saying is, *You're not going to pay **me**, NCAA. You're going to pay **for**. You're going to pay **for** all these facilities. You're going to pay **for** the new generation of sports education. UNC, you're going to pay ten million dollars **for** not only the fraudulent education I received, but **for** all the other athletes coming forward.*

In the documentary *$chooled*, Harvey Perlman, then Chancellor of the University of Nebraska at Lincoln, states, "Student-athletes coming into a university, they know the deal. They're receiving a scholarship in exchange for their athletic ability. If they don't like the deal they should decide to do something else."[85] Mr. Perlman's statement goes back to what I said earlier about certain football coaches' attitude: *If you want to be a scholar, you should work fucking harder. You're not here to be a fucking scholar, you're here to make it to the NFL. You're here to be in the NBA. I don't want to hear about your need to go to study hall or any of that shit. You should've taken your ass to Yale or Harvard if you want to be a scholar. This is a school for athletes.*

The NFL and NBA know that athlete-students are being pushed through the educational system at the university level. They attempt to self-correct what's been done to the athlete-student during college through player development programs and supplemental education programs, but it's often too little too late. I ask, what specialized

84 https://www.sbnation.com/college-basketball/2014/7/8/5880765/rashad-mccants-north-carolina-scandal-ncaa-payments

85 https://www.amazon.com/Schooled-College-Sports-Sam-Rockwell/dp/B00GM2MSGY

education are you giving the athlete that's going to help them in sports and beyond sports; regular education for an athlete doesn't accomplish that because we live in a totally different industry. The athletic world is a subculture because we're not *regular* people. We're being idolized and we're being put on pedestals as role models; we've been catapulted into stardom. The expectations are different. That's why, when you're talking about education and professional sports organizations giving us some type of education, the questions come. What *kind* of education are current pro athletes given?

Dr. Bright states, "I would like to see more majoring in subjects for in-demand fields in this economy. A lot of the time athlete-students end up majoring in African-American studies, and there's not a big demand for that in the labor market. A lot of schools offer vague majors like liberal arts but they're so vague you can put together 120 credits of anything. French literature isn't going to serve the black athlete in the marketplace most likely. A more rigorous preparation process would make these guys economically viable off the field and off the court. It doesn't have to be majoring in computer engineering; it can be majoring in or equipping them in something that's going to make them more economically viable. You can't ignore the reality of the labor market. There has to be a Plan B, C, D, and E in place because most athlete-students will not go professional."[86]

Paid to Play

The argument about whether to pay student-athletes has been going on for decades. I believe the rules and regulations should be completely thrown out, and athletes should be paid to play...period. There should be a definite revenue share amongst all athletes. Michael Hausfeld had this to say: "We're beginning to see the results from the decision in O'Bannon. Athletes really were in a vise and they suffered

---

[86] Personal interview with Dr. Marcus Bright.

two forms of wrong. They were robbed, for the most part, of a quality education. And they were robbed of a share in the revenue built based on their athletic performance and abilities. The O'Bannon case addressed the latter. Rashanda's case addresses the former. So now we see that athletes are achieving at least a measure of increase in what they receive as a result of the commitment to play ball at these schools; as well as the schools responding by increasing the educational opportunities and quality of academics offered to those athletes. It's not anywhere near where it should be but it's a beginning."[87]

According to Dr. Marcus Bright, players are "producing inordinate sums of money to educational institutions and their families in large part come from poverty, living in trailers, living in very tough conditions. Their families are not being compensated, yet you have Nick Saban making ten million dollars a year. And a running back has to take a beating for three years, for what? The compensation of an inferior education?"

Joseph Forte says, "Some level of compensation must be present, whether it's financial or in the form of a trust."[88]

Look how the "paid to play" scenario compares to nonathlete students. Say an English major writes a bestselling novel. There would be no restrictions on the student-author receiving profits from book sales simply because English was the planned major. The same would be true of an engineering student who develops and patents a revolutionary product while in school. These students would receive profits from marketing their skills. Why should athletes be held to a different standard? The answer lies in the almighty dollar generated by athlete-students in the "scholarship for compensation" theory.[89]

---

[87] Personal interview with Michael Hausfeld.
[88] Personal interview with Joseph Forte.
[89] https://digitalcommons.law.byu.edu/cgi/viewcontent.cgi?article=1065&context=elj

Joseph Forte reiterates, "Paying players will take away the whole slavery aspect, the subliminal slave-owner relationship between players and coaches."[90]

Sonny Vaccaro agrees: "It's interesting, because the people who are playing have been the ones who have been induced, and I use that as opposed to recruited; there's billions and billions of dollars made, and they're splitting up the money among themselves. And if they want to use the word 'scholarship,' let's not give players a scholarship. Let's let everybody pay their way if they want to go play football or basketball. That's fine. Because, in reality, if you just listen to what I'm going to say here, that would be a fair equation to me, because the ones who really want to play are the ones who would have access to sign the Nike deals, the adidas deals, the Gatorade deals, and whatever. Let them monetize themselves and let them play."[91]

Mary Willingham concludes, "The one thing I want to make sure is that people know education is important to me, and every day I look at Nelson Mandela's quote about education: 'It's the most powerful weapon which you can use to change the world.' I do want these young people to have an education, but I want it to be their choice, and I want it to be real. So it's not that I don't want to just say, Oh, college athletes should just be paid and they shouldn't get anything else. I think they should have access to the education. It's so important. Because we know that education is the only thing that breaks the cycle of poverty. So you've got to have one generation educated to pull yourself and your family out. So I hope that is people's takeaway from what I had to say."

Players to Coaches

Joseph Forte asserts, "For sports predominantly played by black players, let those players advance to coaching. Look to incor-

---

90   Personal interview with Joseph Forte.
91   Personal interview with Sonny Vaccaro.

porate more students into coaching careers. They [universities and the NCAA] don't want to give the impression that the black male can lead. Their sentiment is: yes, let him be the assistant, the associate, but not the head coach; and by the way, they have to make it look as nonracial as possible."[92]

Shannon Ryan, in a 2016 *Chicago Tribune* article[93] states, "The National Association for Coaching Equity and Development... that represents minority coaches has proposed that the NCAA adopt a version of the NFL's Rooney Rule."

Ryan continues, "Last April, while reporting on the lack of black coaches in men's college basketball, every coach I spoke to told me he didn't want to be hired simply because of his race. They just wanted to see qualified black candidates get a fair shot."

Stand as a United Front

Sonny Vaccaro expresses the sentiment, "It [college athletics as we know it] would all be over tomorrow if ever we had a group of athletes who would stand up against the NCAA. We have athletes stand up against the flag, we have athletes stand up against statues, we have a lot of athletes, but not enough, who have pride in their life, their country, where they are, but all of them are afraid to go against their team or their university. Standing up as one—that's what I would love to see before I die. Don't play in the football playoff, or don't play in the NCAA tournament; at that point I would tell you, from my years of expertise, it would be over tomorrow morning. Why would it be over? Because corporate America, the multibillion-dollar industry that really supports college athletics, would turn on their heels. What good would it be to Nike, or Under Armour, or adidas, to have shoes on somebody who's not playing? They're not doing it for the aesthetic rea-

---

[92]   Personal interview with Joseph Forte.
[93]   With number of black head coaches down, NCAA needs its own Rooney Rule

son that they want to save mankind. They're doing it because exactly what I said in 1976, because the people will see them wear the shoes and you'll sell the shoes. You'll sell the drink. That's what it is. I would love to have a sane mind and body to see that happen. If I had a bucket list I would pray that I live to see the day that the athletes stand up and say screw you, we're not going to play. It's got to be done in front of the world. Make your statement in front of a national audience. Just one time. One team. It would all change tomorrow."[94]

According to Ed O'Bannon, "What's going to make changes, in my opinion, is that the athletes themselves have to force change. How do they do that? They have to come together—there's strength in numbers. Student-athletes need to get on the same page, show some leadership, and sit at the table with the NCAA, lock eyes and say, 'We're not budging until changes are made. Either enact new rules or we'll take our situation to the law.'"[95]

Equip and Empower Parents with Knowledge

Since a high percentage of college athletes are from distressed neighborhoods, the inner city, and underserved communities, it's crucial to educate parents about NCAA rules and violations, and how to push the university to pay for the remainder of their son or daughter's college education if he or she gets injured. The university will try to get away with anything if it can. There needs to be a hard push for parents to be more involved in their kids' education from a young age. As previously discussed, a lot of parents think of their child as a lottery ticket, so once their kid is signed to a university scholarship, the parents think, *That's it, my job is done. The university will take care of everything from here*. No! Athlete-student advocates need to be assigned to each family, to go through the highlights of the hefty 534-page NCAA manual, pointing out

---

[94]   Personal interview with Sonny Vaccaro.
[95]   Personal interview with Ed O'Bannon.

covert rules and violations that could adversely affect their kid, and ultimately bring embarrassment to the family.

Mary Willingham states, "The athlete's parents also see the potential dream. So the whole family participates in the dream that their kid is going to be the family's ticket out of poverty. I get the sense that it's more when families are closer to communities where there is so much emphasis on sports; they see the access that the athletes get, and they hang on to that like it's really going to be the ticket out for them, and they really focus on the athleticism, and parents don't worry too much about the education. I don't think they necessarily make the connection that you have to be prepared to go to college. I think some people who didn't go to college themselves, and maybe didn't make it through high school, see it more as you'll get to go if you're an athlete. So just be an athlete and you'll get to go to college and they'll take care of you. So I think some of it is just a lack of understanding and a lack of education. But some of it is promoted, kind of like the NCAA and the propaganda machine. Some of it is promoted by us, by the people who really believe that a college scholarship is the greatest thing ever. This is why parents need to educate themselves on what educational and athletic path their kid is going to take, and get the full picture of everything involved."

David Bly, member of the Minnesota House of Representatives, District 20B, sums it up: "Your children will become what you are; so be what you want them to be."[96]

---

[96]   http://whatwillmatter.com/2012/10/quote-so-be-what-you-want-them-to-be-david-bly/

EPILOGUE

Since I started writing this book, new disclosures about academic and athletic scandal and fraud have been streaked across the airwaves like oil paint smeared on a canvas.

First, we witnessed the confession of Jay Williams, recruiter for Ceruzzi Sports and Entertainment. Williams admitted to funneling two hundred and fifty thousand dollars to Kevin Love's AAU coach, Pat Barrett, while serving as a representative for the sports agency.[97]

Then we watched while more news blew up, including this from a 2017 *SportingNews* article: "The widespread and ongoing federal investigation into bribery and fraud in college basketball, which led to an adidas executive's arrest Tuesday, apparently is now spreading to Nike."[98] Nike Elite Youth Basketball League (EYBL) employees did not escape the scrutiny with its grassroots division employees, along with pertinent documents subpoenaed by the

---

[97] http://ftw.usatoday.com/2017/09/espn-jay-williams-kevin-love-aau-coach-250-college-basketball-scandal-fbi-ncaa

[98] http://www.sportingnews.com/ncaa-basketball/news/nike-justice-department-fbi-college-basketball-coach-arrests/1k5n2el7howse10l0a3c-b57wdw

FBI for further examination. To support the claim,[99] SBNation reported in 2017: "Nike does have a connection to all of this: Merl Code, an adidas employee arrested on Tuesday, formerly worked for Nike. Nike college programs like Arizona, Oklahoma State, and USC also had assistant coaches who were arrested and charged in the probe."

The arrests sent ripples of shock through the Division I men's basketball coaching world. Jim Gatto, Director of Sports Marketing for adidas, and four assistant coaches at Division I basketball programs, were among those arrested. Longtime coach Rick Pitino got the ax from Louisville.

We shouldn't be surprised that the Justice Department (FBI) uncovered a far-reaching system of bribery and fraud as it relates to financial advisors, the system of fraud and scandal that has been embedded in the collegiate world for decades.

People most often associate shady transactions with schools that recruit players who are at-risk, but that's not at all true. Shady transactions have happened and will continue to happen across the U.S., with the most prestigious of universities experiencing, as Willingham and Smith put it, "embarrassing misconduct carried out for the benefit of athletes." We're talking UNC, Duke, UCLA, Auburn, University of Washington, University of Michigan, and all the rest, too many to name here, including at the professional level.

Another example[100] that sent seismic shock waves throughout the country was when the NCAA proclaimed in 2017 that *no sanctions would be handed out to UNC*. They deemed the decades of fraudulent classes to be an academic problem, not an athletic one,

---

[99]   https://www.sbnation.com/college-basketball/2017/9/27/16375138/nike-eybl-fbi-college-basketball-scandal

[100]   https://amp-newsobservercom.cdn.ampproject.org/c/amp.newsobserver.com/news/local/education/unc-scandal/article183717756.html

and therefore claimed no violations occurred. The headliner: the NCAA Committee on Infractions released a long-awaited judgment in which it "could not conclude academic violations in the case." The McClatchy Video Lab displayed, "The Committee did not sanction the institution with any significant penalties."[101]

In handing down its ruling, the NCAA conveniently ignored the long-standing "shadow curriculum" of classes instituted in 1993 by Debbie Crowder that pushed over 3,100 athlete-students through the university system to keep them eligible. In 2012, former North Carolina Governor Jim Martin called the scandal "an isolated academic scandal," later admitting it was indeed an athletic scandal. In 2014, the Wainstein Report confirmed eighteen years of fake classes over a course of two decades. Rob J. Anderson, in his 2014 book *Tarnished Heels,* concludes his detailed account: "After nearly four years of scandals there ultimately are very few definitive answers. Not because of a lack of evidence, but rather due to an obstinate lack of cooperation and openness by UNC."

On October 16, 2017, *The News and Observer*[102] reported, "UNC-Chapel Hill's accrediting body has declined to take further action after reviewing the NCAA report that last week issued no punishment against the university for its long-running athletic and academic scandal." UNC has reportedly spent upwards of twenty-one million dollars defending itself against the NCAA's allegations.

---

[101] http://www.newsobserver.com/news/local/education/unc-scandal/article183717756.html

[102] Tarnished Heels: *How Unethical Actions and Deliberate Deceit at the University of North Carolina Ended "The Carolina Way"* http://amp.newsobserver.com/news/local/education/article179169576.html?utm_medium=referral&utm_campaign=amp&utm_source=www.newsobserver.com-RelayMediaAMP

All these latest reports support the premise of this book. I will stand up and take my beating at the whipping post of truth for refusing to say my slave name of *athlete-student*. I'm not okay with that title as long as it carries the scars of lack of education, a repressed future, and a marginalized existence. I'm fucking mad that athlete-students continue to bear the generational brunt of scandal and fraud.

They're the true victims and unless some radical reforms take place, they will continue to experience plantation education.

A FINAL WORD

What I've told you in this book demands action. It demands that you make a decision.

Today. Right now.

You have no choice but to make a choice.

You know in the deepest recesses of your conscience you've already made your decision, but I challenge you head-on to consider the long-term effects of that decision. How will your decision affect the youth in your family, in your neighborhood, in your workplace, and in the generations to come?

Will you continue to be psychologically controlled because the price of taking action outweighs the cost of staying marginalized?

Will you refuse to be a part of redefining the social and cultural force that prevails in our country?

Will you continue to allow universities, the NCAA, and sleek marketers to capitalize on your skin color so they can sell a bridge from the inner city to Madison Avenue?

According to Jim Knight, then-news columnist in 2008 for *Ann Arbor* (Michigan) *News,*[103] "Unless you've drunk the Everything's OK Kool-Aid, you're viewed as an adversary."

---

[103] "University of Michigan buries scrutiny of athletes' academics," June 15, 2008

Willingham and Smith continue the sentiment: "Too many powerful people on too many big-time sport campuses have become silent partners in a plot to defraud. Having convinced themselves of the fundamental virtues of college sport, and of their own underlying probity, they work to deflect critical attention from practices whose ugly realities cannot be spoken out loud."[104]

In the epic TV movie series from the 1970s, *Roots* (which was just a watered-down version of what really happened to make it palatable for white people to watch), one of the last segments summarizes exactly what the NCAA, universities, and athletic departments across the country have perpetrated on athlete-students. In one scene, Tom, the great-great-grandson of Kunte Kinte, is giving a speech in a barn immediately after the Civil War ends. He says, and I paraphrase: "How are we going to feed our children? Put a roof over our heads? We're all ignorant and that's exactly what the masters wanted. We haven't been taught enough to earn a living in the white man's world. If we ever plan to leave here, we had better learn how to take care of ourselves first."

William C. Rhoden says it well: "As deep and rich as their history has been, black athletes have failed to produce a leader who understood the potential of this black athletic nation to join in the larger push for freedom. That's because, in their own world, by their own definition, black athletes already were 'free.' Unfortunately, the terms of liberation have always been defined by the white men who were responsible for their wealth. When Pharaoh defines your Promised Land, you can bet you'll never find it."[105]

Don't shout out proudly that you're a rebel because you feel strongly about what you believe in. The only way I will acknowl-

---

[104] Excerpt from book, Cheated, by Jay Smith and Mary Willingham [2015]

[105] Excerpt from book, 40 Million Dollar Slaves by William Rhoden [2006]

edge you as part of the rebellion is when your fear and "sunken place" is replaced by action. When you are no longer held by a Willie Lynch slave mentality that cries:

> I can't speak up; *massa* will scorn me.
>
> I can't speak up; friends and family will desert me.
>
> I can't speak up; I'll lose my reputation.
>
> I can't speak up; I'll be psychologically
> and socially lashed by the *massa*.

Willie Lynch's purpose was to produce endless generations imbued with a slave mentality. Plantation education is nothing more than that, played out generationally.

How will I know you still possess a plantation mentality?

You won't exhibit enough self-confidence to speak up.
You won't own enough self-esteem to stand up.
What you will essentially say to your plantation owner is:
Lock me up.
Feed me.
Tell me what to wear.
Tell me what to read.
Tell me when to shower.
Tell me when to piss.
Tell me when to eat.
Tell me what to believe.
Tell me what I want to hear…then rob me of my money.
I don't want to hear anything you have to say unless you're willing to be labeled as crazy, tormented, and insolent.
Unless you're willing to lose everything, shut the fuck up.
For slaves on plantations, freedom was not an option.
It was the only life they knew, the only life they could

accept. They were slaves for life because their mentality was that of a slave.

Rebellion was too frightening, too terrifying, except for people like Nat Turner.

Many today will die on the soil of the modern-day athlete-student plantation, but there will be no physical casket. Rather...

Their souls will die from years of acquiescing to the *system*.

Their minds will die from lack of education.

Their bodies will die a slow death, broken and bruised, on the battlefields of football and basketball, while their captors smugly wave their victory flag crafted from the billions of dollars they have made off the backs of plantation education slaves.

There has always been a price to pay for rebellion. Social rebellion toward the *system*, and personal rebellion within one's conscience when choosing to lead a revolt. I have paid my price, and will continue to pay my price for leading the revolt. The powers-that-be warn rebels, don't be a hero off the court; just shut up and do your work. They're waiting to pounce; they will do everything within their power to invalidate my story. I also know that most of you reading this book will say, *Go for it, Rashad, speak up, stand up, lead the rebellion, put yourself on the firing line, and if it pans out well, we might join you down the road.*

That tells me everything I need to know about you.

The question now begs to be asked:

Are you part of the Plantation?

or...

part of the Rebellion?

APPENDIX A

Rashanda McCants' UNC Transcripts

GEOL 101	INTRODUCTORY GEOL	2006 Fall	B-	3.00
GEOL 101L	INTRODUCTORY GEOL L	2008 Spring	C-	1.00
MUSC 121	FUND OF MUSIC I	2008 Spring	C+	3.00
PHIL .030	APPLIED ETHICS	2005 Summer II	B	3.00
PHIL .047	ETHICS OF SPORT	2006 Summer I	A	3.00
PHIL 275	PHIL ISSU/GENDER	2007 Spring		0.00
PHIL 275	PHIL ISSU/GENDER	2007 Spring	B+	3.00
PHIL 390	SEM SELECTED TOPICS	2009 Spring	B+	3.00
PHIL 560	ETHICS BOWL	2008 Fall	A	3.00
PHYA .001P	REQUIRED ACTIVITES	2006 Spring	PL	1.00
PHYA 221	BEGINNING JOGGING	2009 Spring	B	1.00
PSYC .010	GENERAL PSYCHOLOGY	2006 Spring	C+	3.00
PSYC 260	SOCIAL PSYCHOLOGY	2007 Fall	B	3.00
SOCI .010	SOC PERSPECTIVES	2005 Fall	C+	3.00
SOCI .022	RACE & ETHNIC RELATIONS	2006 Spring	C	3.00
SWAH 112	KISWAHILI 1-2	2007 Summer I	B	6.00
SWAH 403	KISWAHILI 3	2008 Summer II	A-	3.00

RASHAD MCCANTS

Course	Description	Term	Grade	Units	Repe Code
COMM 171	ARGUMENT AND DEBATE	2009 Spring	A	3.00	_
COMM 223	SMALL GROUP COMM	2007 Fall	B	3.00	_
COMM 230	AUD/VID/FLM PRD/WRT	2008 Fall	B+	3.00	_
COMM 312	PERSUASION	2007 Fall	B+	3.00	_
COMM 432	VISUAL CULTURE	2009 Spring	B+	3.00	_
COMM 639	SPEC TOPIC/MED PROD	2008 Summer I	A	3.00	_
COMM 639	SPEC TOPIC/MED PROD	2008 Fall	B+	3.00	_
COMP 380	COMPUTERS & SOCIETY	2008 Spring		0.00	_
COMP 380	COMPUTERS & SOCIETY	2008 Spring	B	3.00	_
DRAM 116	PERSP IN THE THEATRE	2007 Spring	C	3.00	_
DRAM 140	VOICE TRAINING I	2008 Spring	B	3.00	_
EDUC 441	EDUC IN AM SOCIETY	2008 Fall	B+	3.00	_
ENGL .010	BASIC WRITING	2005 Summer II	B-	3.00	_
ENGL .011	ENG COMP & RHETORIC	2005 Fall	B	3.00	_
ENGL .012	ENG COMP & RHETORIC	2006 Spring	B+	3.00	_
EXSS .041	PERSONAL HEALTH	2005 Fall	C	3.00	_
GEOG 121	PEOPLE AND PLACES	2006 Fall	B	3.00	_

🟢 Taken   ⬅Transferred   ◆ In Progress

Course	Description	Term	Grade	Units	Repe Code
AFAM .006K	1ST YEAR SEM FINE ARTS	2006 Spring	B-	3.00	_
AFAM .041	BLACK EXPERIENCE	2005 Fall	A-	3.00	_
AFAM .065	TOPICS IN AFAM STUD	2006 Spring	B+	3.00	_
AFAM 101	BLACK EXPERIENCE I	2006 Fall	B	3.00	_
AFAM 276	BLACKS IN FILM	2006 Fall	B	3.00	_
AFRI 520	SOUTHERN AFRICA	2008 Spring	A-	3.00	_
COMM .013	PUBLIC SPEAKING	2006 Summer I	A	3.00	_
COMM 120	INTRO INTERPER/ORG COMM	2007 Spring	C+	3.00	_
COMM 130	INTRO MEDIA PROD	2007 Fall	A-	3.00	_
COMM 130	INTRO MEDIA PROD	2007 Fall		0.00	_
COMM 140	INTRO MED HIST/THEO/CRIT	2008 Summer II	B+	3.00	_
COMM 142	POPULAR MUSIC	2009 Spring	A-	3.00	_
COMM 160	INTRO PERFORM ST/LIT	2007 Spring	A-	3.00	_

PLANTATION EDUCATION

Connect
CAROLINAshanda Mccants, Welcome!   Home

Find | View All   1 of 1

Seq Nbr 1
ID 711504635   Rashanda Mccants

Internal Unofficial Transcript - UNC Chapel Hill

Name   : Rashanda Mccants

Student ID: 711504635

Print Date : 2017-12-06

- - - - - **Degrees Awarded** - - - - -

Degree   : Bachelor of Arts

Confer Date   : 2009-05-10

Degree GPA   : 3.119

Plan   : College of Arts and Sciences

              Communication Studies

Sub-Plan   : Communication Studies: Media Studies/Production

- - - - - **Academic Program History** - - - - -

Program   : AS Bachelor

2005-06-22 : Active in Program

              2005-06-22 : Business Administration Major

2005-08-29 : Active in Program

              2005-08-29 : Undecided Major

2007-01-09 : Active in Program

              2007-01-09 : Communication Studies Major

Program   : AS Bachelor of Arts

2007-05-14 : Active in Program

- - - - Degrees Awarded - - - -

Degree   : Bachelor of Arts

Confer Date : 2009-05-10

Degree GPA   : 3.119

Plan   : College of Arts and Sciences

                Communication Studies

Sub-Plan   : Communication Studies: Media Studies/Production

- - - - - Academic Program History - - - - -

Program   : AS Bachelor

2005-06-22   : Active in Program

                2005-06-22 : Business Administration Major

2005-08-29   : Active in Program

                2005-08-29 : Undecided Major

2007-01-09   : Active in Program

                2007-01-09 : Communication Studies Major

Program   : AS Bachelor of Arts

2007-05-14   : Active in Program

                2007-05-14 : Communication Studies Major

- - - - - Beginning of Undergraduate Record - - - - -

2005 SumII

| ENGL | .010 | BASIC WRITING | 3.00 | 3.00 B- | 8.100 |
| PHIL | .030 | APPLIED ETHICS | 3.00 | 3.00 B | 9.000 |

        TERM GPA :   2.850   TERM TOTALS :   6.00   6.00   17.100

        CUM GPA :   2.850   CUM TOTALS :   6.00   6.00   17.100

                Good Standing

2005 Fall

AFAM	.041	BLACK EXPERIENCE	3.00	3.00 A-	11.100
ENGL	.011	ENG COMP & RHETORIC	3.00	3.00 B	9.000
EXSS	.041	PERSONAL HEALTH	3.00	3.00 C	6.000

2008 SumII

COMM	140	INTRO MED HIST/THEO/CRIT	3.00	3.00	B+	9.900
SWAH	403	KISWAHILI 3	3.00	3.00	A-	11.100

TERM GPA :   3.500   TERM TOTALS :   6.00   6.00   21.000

CUM   GPA :   3.025   CUM   TOTALS :   104.00   103.00   311.600

Good Standing

2008 Fall

COMM	230	AUD/VID/FLM PRD/WRT	3.00	3.00	B+	9.900
COMM	639	SPEC TOPIC/MED PROD	3.00	3.00	B+	9.900

Course Topic(s): WRITING THE 1 HR DRAMA

EDUC	441	EDUC IN AM SOCIETY	3.00	3.00	B+	9.900
PHIL	560	ETHICS BOWL	3.00	3.00	A	12.000

TERM GPA :   3.475   TERM TOTALS :   12.00   12.00   41.700

CUM   GPA :   3.072   CUM   TOTALS :   116.00   115.00   353.300

Good Standing

2009 Spr

COMM	142	POPULAR MUSIC	3.00	3.00	A-	11.100
COMM	171	ARGUMENT AND DEBATE	3.00	3.00	A	12.000
COMM	432	VISUAL CULTURE	3.00	3.00	B+	9.900
PHIL	390	SEM SELECTED TOPICS	3.00	3.00	B+	9.900
PHYA	221	BEGINNING JOGGING	1.00	0.00	B	

Grading Basis: EXCLUDE FROM HRS TO GRADUATION

TERM GPA :   3.531   TERM TOTALS :   13.00   12.00   45.900

CUM   GPA :   3.119   CUM   TOTALS :   129.00   127.00   399.200

Dean's List

Good Standing

Cancel

2007 Spr

COMM	120	INTRO INTERPER/ORG COMM	3.00	3.00 C+	6.900
COMM	160	INTRO PERFORM ST/LIT	3.00	3.00 A-	11.100
DRAM	116	PERSP IN THE THEATRE	3.00	3.00 C	6.000
PHIL	275	PHIL ISSU/GENDER	3.00	3.00 B+	9.900

TERM GPA :   2.825   TERM TOTALS :   12.00   12.00   33.900

CUM GPA :   2.919   CUM TOTALS :   64.00   63.00   183.900

Good Standing

2007 SumI

SWAH	112	KISWAHILI 1-2	6.00	6.00 B	18.000

TERM GPA :   3.000   TERM TOTALS :   6.00   6.00   18.000

CUM GPA :   2.926   CUM TOTALS :   70.00   69.00   201.900

Good Standing

2007 Fall

COMM	130	INTRO MEDIA PROD	3.00	3.00 A-	11.100
COMM	223	SMALL GROUP COMM	3.00	3.00 B	9.000
COMM	312	PERSUASION	3.00	3.00 B+	9.900
PSYC	260	SOCIAL PSYCHOLOGY	3.00	3.00 B	9.000

TERM GPA :   3.250   TERM TOTALS :   12.00   12.00   39.000

CUM GPA :   2.974   CUM TOTALS :   82.00   81.00   240.900

Good Standing

2008 Spr

AFRI	520	SOUTHERN AFRICA	3.00	3.00 A-	11.100
COMP	380	COMPUTERS & SOCIETY	3.00	3.00 B	9.000
DRAM	140	VOICE TRAINING I	3.00	3.00 B	9.000
GEOL	101L	INTRODUCTORY GEOL L	1.00	1.00 C-	1.700
MUSC	121	FUND OF MUSIC I	3.00	3.00 C+	6.900

CUM GPA : 2.703   CUM TOTALS : 18.00   18.00   50.100

Good Standing

2006 Spr

AFAM	.006K	1ST YEAR SEM FINE ARTS	3.00	3.00 B-	8.100

Course Topic(s): RACE IN CINEMA

AFAM	.065	TOPICS IN AFAM STUD	3.00	3.00 B+	9.900
ENGL	.012	ENG COMP & RHETORIC	3.00	3.00 B+	9.900
PHYA	.001P	REQUIRED ACTIVITES	1.00	0.00 PL	
PSYC	.010	GENERAL PSYCHOLOGY	3.00	3.00 C+	6.900
SOCI	.022	RACE & ETHNIC RELATIONS	3.00	3.00 C	6.000

TERM GPA : 2.720   TERM TOTALS : 16.00   15.00   40.800

CUM GPA : 2.755   CUM TOTALS : 34.00   33.00   90.900

Good Standing

2006 SumI

COMM	.013	PUBLIC SPEAKING	3.00	3.00 A	12.000
PHIL	.047	ETHICS OF SPORT	3.00	3.00 A	12.000

TERM GPA : 4.000   TERM TOTALS : 6.00   6.00   24.000

CUM GPA : 2.946   CUM TOTALS : 40.00   39.00   114.900

Good Standing

2006 Fall

AFAM	101	BLACK EXPERIENCE I	3.00	3.00 B	9.000
AFAM	276	BLACKS IN FILM	3.00	3.00 B	9.000
GEOG	121	PEOPLE AND PLACES	3.00	3.00 B	9.000
GEOL	101	INTRODUCTORY GEOL	3.00	3.00 B-	8.100

TERM GPA : 2.925   TERM TOTALS : 12.00   12.00   35.100

CUM GPA : 2.941   CUM TOTALS : 52.00   51.00   150.000

Good Standing

RASHAD MCCANTS

2007-05-14 : Communication Studies Major

- - - - - **Beginning of Undergraduate Record** - - - - -

2005 SumII

ENGL	.010	BASIC WRITING	3.00	3.00 B-	8.100
PHIL	.030	APPLIED ETHICS	3.00	3.00 B	9.000

TERM GPA :   2.850   TERM TOTALS :   6.00   6.00   17.100

CUM GPA :   2.850   CUM TOTALS :   6.00   6.00   17.100

Good Standing

2005 Fall

AFAM	.041	BLACK EXPERIENCE	3.00	3.00 A-	11.100
ENGL	.011	ENG COMP & RHETORIC	3.00	3.00 B	9.000
EXSS	.041	PERSONAL HEALTH	3.00	3.00 C	6.000
SOCI	.010	SOC PERSPECTIVES	3.00	3.00 C+	6.900

TERM GPA :   2.750   TERM TOTALS :   12.00   12.00   33.000

CUM GPA :   2.783   CUM TOTALS :   18.00   18.00   50.100

Good Standing

2006 Spr

AFAM	.006K	1ST YEAR SEM FINE ARTS	3.00	3.00 B-	8.100

   Course Topic(s): RACE IN CINEMA

AFAM	.065	TOPICS IN AFAM STUD	3.00	3.00 B+	9.900
ENGL	.012	ENG COMP & RHETORIC	3.00	3.00 B+	9.900
PHYA	.001P	REQUIRED ACTIVITES	1.00	0.00 PL	
PSYC	.010	GENERAL PSYCHOLOGY	3.00	3.00 C+	6.900
SOCI	.022	RACE & ETHNIC RELATIONS	3.00	3.00 C	6.000

TERM GPA :   2.720   TERM TOTALS :   16.00   15.00   40.800

CUM GPA :   2.755   CUM TOTALS :   34.00   33.00   90.900

Good Standing

194

ACKNOWLEDGMENTS

I would like to take this time to thank the people who helped me get this far to accomplish this extraordinary feat. These people all played a part in this book becoming what it is and keeping me alive and full of spirit to push through the toughest times of my life.

- James Keith
- Michael Moore
- Jerell Hill
- Cole Patterson
- Precious Wilson
- Omar Wilson
- Kelsey Gillespie
- Sameka Jones
- Ike Diogu
- Claudia Salazar
- Jeremiah Haylett
- Cameron Maybin
- Jessica Johnson
- Joseph Forte
- Mary Willingham
- Latashia Deveaux
- Dominique Bluette

- Jamall Lovell
- Damont Nickson
- Gregory Ash-Buck
- Pieter Oliver
- Sara Ramaker
- Stephen Jackson
- Martina Kotseva
- Michelle Hill
- Amber Blackwell
- Tyler Salmon

I could have never done any of this without my rock, my twin, my everything: my sister, my soul protector, Rashanda McCants. I could never explain or have enough words to describe our bond. She is everything about what a friend is, and ever could be. No one needs to know what we've been through. We know. Now we are here. It's time to finally watch the world dance to our beat.

ABOUT THE AUTHOR

Rashad Dion McCants (born September 25, 1984) is a former American professional basketball player. McCants began his high school career at Erwin High School in Asheville, North Carolina, but finished at New Hampton (New Hampshire) School. He led New Hampton to the 2002 New England Prep School Class A championship and was named MVP of the title game. Alongside Sean May, Raymond Felton, and David Noel, McCants joined a stellar recruiting class at UNC for the 2002–2003 season, coached by Matt Doherty.

In his freshman year, McCants led the Tar Heels in scoring with 17.5 points per game. McCants scored 1,721 points in his career at North Carolina and made 221 career three-point field goals. After UNC won the NCAA championship, McCants declared his eligibility for the 2005 NBA Draft, and was selected fourteenth overall by the Minnesota Timberwolves. His college teammates, Marvin Williams, Raymond Felton, and Sean May, were also selected in the draft. McCants' sister, Rashanda McCants, played in the WNBA. Rashad is the cousin of Major League Baseball player Cameron Maybin and third cousin of former Canadian Football League player John Avery.

Rashad's last year in the NBA was 2010, and since that time he has been living the California dream in Hollywood, interacting with some of the world's most famous stars and pursuing his goals in music and film. In 2017, Rashad was the first pick for Trilogy, the dominant team that went 10-0 in Ice Cube's three-on-three basketball league's first season.

Rashad's mother and father, James and Brenda McCants, along with younger sister Sade, have been his biggest supporters during his tremendous journey to where he stands now.

Business ventures

YBG Entertainment Group: 2006–2015
Music, film, and event production company that offers a one-stop shop development hub for artist and entertainers alike. Giving independent entertainers the resources needed to perform and experience the entertainment industry.

The Heroes Foundation: 2016
Public charity, aiming to financially aid and advise athletes and entertainers. We provide scholarships and grants for entertainers and athletes to perform without the financial worries of housing, transportation, food, studio, gym time, photo shoots, music videos, etc.

Kobe Jordan productions: 2016
Music production hub where artists, songwriters, producers, and engineers collaborate to create new music for emerging and current artists. Our hub is a publishing cash cow with talented songwriters and producers who deliver top quality product. For artists who show star potential in the music industry and want a shot at the big leagues, Kobe Jordan is the company that puts the artist in the game.

Reign & Associates: 2016
Entertainment consulting company
Aims to advise and consult entertainers in business development, talent development, event production, wealth and investment consulting, and lifestyle branding and marketing.

Dashletics Elite Training: 2016
Personal player development training for athletes and youth
Skills for eight to thirty years old. Ball handling, sharp shooting, defense, strength and conditioning, and film sessions. Ultimately, Dashletics' purpose is to be the premier training academy for all athletes of USAE (see below), The Heroes Foundation, and Reign & Associates.

United Society for Athlete Education (USAE): 2015
Coalition for athletes to help develop sports education as a certified degree and career path. Strategically-developed high school curriculums with performance-based requirements should allow athletes to get a step ahead in sports education and information about their respective sports lifestyle and culture. USAE is a nonprofit that is geared around legislative change for education reform. USAE is also pushing for the eradication of academic requirements for athletes and opening the door for employee compensation for athletes as compared to coaches. If coaches are employees, the players are employees too. (Mary Willingham project)

The Legacy Center (TLC): 2014
Sports education international university
One hundred million-dollar sports facility project that includes dormitories, auditorium, café, fitness center, rehabilitation center, classrooms, multipurpose courts and fields, locker rooms, swimming pools, steam rooms, day care center, and much more. The

ultimate one-stop shop information hub for athletes and those pursuing a career in sports. The goal is to create four hubs (California, Texas, Georgia, and Ohio) and monetize the athletes who want sports education and a better outlook on the business and lifestyle of their sport. The TLC will generate huge profit for the branding and preparation of young athletes, and that profit will go into the development of the athletes into high-quality, knowledgeable business people.